Gingham Aprons
of the '40s & '50s

A Checkered Past

Judy Florence

Schiffer Publishing Ltd®

4880 Lower Valley Road, Atglen, PA 19310 USA

Copyright © 2003 by Judy Florence
Library of Congress Control Number: 2002115126

Designed by Bonnie M. Hensley
Cover design by Bruce M. Waters
Type set in University Roman Bd BT / Souvenir Lt BT

ISBN: 0-7643-1748-2
Printed in China
1 2 3 4

Published by Schiffer Publishing Ltd.
4880 Lower Valley Road
Atglen, PA 19310
Phone: (610) 593-1777; Fax: (610) 593-2002
E-mail: Schifferbk@aol.com
Please visit our web site catalog at **www.schifferbooks.com**

In Europe, Schiffer books are distributed by Bushwood Books
6 Marksbury Avenue Kew Gardens
Surrey TW9 4JF England
Phone: 44 (0) 20-8392-8585; Fax: 44 (0) 20-8392-9876
E-mail: Bushwd@aol.com
Free postage in the UK. Europe: air mail at cost.

This book may be purchased from the publisher.
Include $3.95 for shipping. Please try your bookstore first.
We are always looking for people to write books on new and related subjects.
If you have an idea for a book please contact us at the above address.
You may write for a free catalog.

Dedication

For you, Dave.

Acknowledgments

Thanks to Janet Carson, Dorothy Gilbertson, Jan Holte, Dorothy McMenomy, Vivian Mets, Lois Osterberg, Eilene Paulson, Pat Schoen, Pat Simonsen, Sherry Stuve, Betty Wilson, and Terri Wyman for sharing aprons, patterns, books, information, and ideas.

Special thanks to Jim Simonsen for hours of dedication to the photography for this book. His expertise with a camera and lighting are the perfect complement to my efforts with a steam iron on gingham aprons.

Contents

Preface

My first book about aprons, titled *Aprons of the Mid-20th Century: To Serve and Protect,* was released in the summer of 2001. It was the result of my growing fascination with aprons, which began in 1995 when I started what has become a rather substantial collection of these humble household textiles.

The first chapter of that book was devoted to *gingham* aprons, one of the most popular styles of the mid-20th century. Fifteen examples were included, each a different color. I had collected gingham aprons in red, pink, orange, yellow, light green, dark green, turquoise, light blue, dark blue, lavender, purple, beige, brown, gray, and black. All fifteen were constructed from 1/8 inch gingham checks, and all boasted a decorative hand cross stitched design and one patch pocket.

Those 'final fifteen' were merely a sample (about one-tenth) of my personal collection of gingham aprons. The only thing about ginghams I had thoroughly presented was the available color range in 'eight checks per inch' fabric. Dozens of additional gingham aprons remained in my closet, yet to be studied and photographed. Clearly there was a lot more to be investigated.

And so I ventured deeper into this 'checkered past', never anticipating the result would be a book with fourteen chapters devoted exclusively to gingham aprons—chapters covering far more than mere checks and little X's. There are chapters that feature a myriad of designs, some unpretentious, others complicated; some are serious while others are whimsical. Another chapter features rectangles, squares, triangles, and diamonds while still others are about stars and flowers, kittens and butterflies, trees and acorns, prayers and blessings. And that's just in the cross stitch section!

Add to that a host of other gingham apron design techniques such as miniature and jumbo rickrack decoration, metallic rickrack design, pulled thread patterns, smocking, Teneriffe lace, and stairstep borders and we have several more chapters. Oddities such as convertible, printed, and drawstring aprons, and styles with organdy, appliqué, and crocheted edging make up an entire section of their own.

Because the majority of gingham aprons are handmade, I find them particularly intriguing. As an experienced hand quiltmaker, I have always appreciated the artistry of hand needlework. I am well aware of the time and

skills required for fine handmade textiles. Most gingham aprons reflect this devotion of time and talent, and I have commented on the presence and amount of handwork in many of the apron descriptions.

Because I have spent decades creating handmade textiles and because I have witnessed the decline in both the production and appreciation of hand needle arts, I place a very high value on them. A large portion of the impetus for writing this book has to do with my hope to increase the reader's awareness of handmade household textiles.

When people found out I was writing my *first* book about aprons, the usual responses were either a puzzled look (*why* aprons?), or a yawn (*ho-hum*). That was about two years ago. Now when I mention that I am working on another book manuscript they ask 'about what?' When I say 'about aprons', the response is '*another* book about aprons?' (Implied, 'surely all of what could be said about aprons could be said in *one* book.) Not true—here's proof that the minimum requirement is at least two books. Don't tell the skeptics that two or three additional books about aprons are lurking in the back of my head. (When I was writing books about quiltmaking, it took *seven* titles before I decided to change subjects.)

I have discovered that since publication of *Aprons of the Mid-20th Century: To Serve and Protect,* far fewer people scoff at the mention of my research and writing interests. I find this encouraging and believe I am being taken more seriously. If nothing else, the first book increased awareness of the world of aprons and household textiles. I am pleased to report that aprons have 'gone national!' Television shows, gallery exhibitions, sewing contests, and museum workshops have been devoted to aprons. I have found evidence of aprons in recent magazines, catalogs, newsletters, books, *and* the weekly television listings. For the past several months, the daily newspaper of a nearby large city has devoted portions of a column to dialogue among readers reminiscing about their mom's aprons and all the memories attached to them! From the Smithsonian to the Senior Citizens Center, people are noticing aprons.

The chapters ahead are filled with the artistry of gingham aprons I have spent many months collecting, laundering, ironing, examining, documenting, photographing, and fondling. I hope you enjoy them.

Judy Florence

Introduction
The World of Aprons

An Update

Since I began seriously collecting and researching the American Apron in 1995, I have witnessed a steady growth of interest in many of the 'humble' household linens. Aprons are gaining in status in the collectible household textiles department! People are finally paying attention to these 'pieces of the past'. Along with colorful handkerchiefs, printed tablecloths, and vintage kitchen towels, aprons are increasing in both personal regard and monetary value. Entire books, magazine articles, major exhibitions, and television shows have been devoted to these household textiles.

Aprons have attained collectible status for a number of reasons. First is the nostalgia factor. Men and women alike are looking back thirty, forty, fifty, or sixty years with increased sentimentality. What was common and routine, perhaps even uninteresting, gradually (or, sometimes suddenly) becomes intriguing when viewed across the span of a generation or two. What was formerly regarded as 'ordinary' becomes 'extraordinary'. The 'retro' look in wearables and decorating is extremely popular. Simplicity, McCall's, and Butterick pattern companies now include a 'retro collection' of apron patterns in their catalogs.

The intrigue of domesticity also plays a part in the rising status of aprons as collectibles. Whether scorned or revered, domesticity

A portion of the Judy Florence's collection of gingham aprons, ready for study, photography, and display.

and all that it connotes is a popular cultural phenomenon. Recent issues of popular and widely circulated women's home and garden magazines have featured advertisements portraying women in stereotypical housewife roles. This was common in the 1930s, 40s, 50s, and 60s. But to see it fifty years later is something of a surprise. The March 2001 issue of *Better Homes and Gardens* magazine carried an advertisement for Armstrong flooring. Poised front and center in a retro style kitchen with SpatterDash-Style vinyl flooring is a curly-haired young woman. She is wearing a blouse with roll up sleeves, capri pants, flats, *and* an apron. And it's not your ordinary apron. It has contrasting fabrics, a designer waistband, and plenty of rickrack trim.

Further evidence of the fascination with 'domesticity' extends beyond the printed page. Textile artists and quitmakers have expressed their views and opinions with colorful pieces that incorporate apron designs, apron fabrics, and recycled aprons. The interpretations and renditions range from sentimental to shocking. I was recently invited to participate in a 'domesticity' theme art show at a regional library. Each artist was asked to express his or her personal reflection of household life, housework, the meaning of home, or any other topic related to domesticity, past or present. Although the ways to express domesticity are vast, aprons are certainly an obvious and popular medium for doing so.

We in the world of textile collecting and conservation always knew that aprons ranked right up there with baseball, hot dogs, and apple pie. Now they can claim a rightful and deserved place alongside lace, linens, and other fine textiles.

A Closer Look

An in-depth look at the world of aprons as pictured in the printed media of the past century reveals a surprising number of portrayals. As one might expect, the most common representation is an adult female wearing an apron, usually in the kitchen or dining room. Books, magazines, and catalogs abound with these apron-clad women. Less frequently pictured are girls, boys, and men, in that order.

I have examined many books, including cookbooks, children's storybooks, grammar school reading textbooks, and high school textbooks, looking for pictures of people wearing aprons. I have also scoured catalogs, major ones like Sears, Montgomery Ward, McCalls, and Simplicity and lesser ones like mail order needlework catalogs and sewing machine manuals, in an effort to define and describe the position of the apron in past generations. I have perused old photographs and family albums.

I was mostly pleased and often amused by what I found. Because aprons were such an integral part of my childhood and teenage years, I paid little attention to them at the time. Now as I look at the images of girls, boys, teenagers, men, and women in aprons, I am impressed with the variety and ubiquity. Here are a few of my favorite apron portrayals.

Children and Aprons

Children's aprons were not confined to the kitchen. Aprons were a sensible means of protecting a child's clothing, whatever the activity or task—playtime, gardening, household chores, or helping Mom in the kitchen. Wearing an apron meant a lightened load of laundry.

Some children's aprons, however, were mainly decorative. The style commonly referred to as a 'pinafore' was worn over a girl's dress. Often these were quite showy, with thick gathers, many ruffles, and oversize sashes. The young lady pictured on page 20 of the children's book *Growing Pains* wears a sashed white apron over her bright blue puffed sleeve dress. Add white anklets and blue hair ribbons, and the result is a comfortable looking outfit, just right for curling up in with a favorite book.

A girl at play, wearing a protective pinafore over her dress. *At Play*, page 21, ©The John C. Winston Company, 1940.

A young girl with sashed apron. This pinafore style provided a combination of decoration and sensible protection during a child's activities. *Growing Pains*, page 20, ©The Westminster Press, 1948.

Aprons were worn for playtime, too. A light blue pinafore protects the red dress of this fair-haired lass. In an era when all little girls wore dresses and all mothers spent many hours of their week doing the family laundry, protection of clothing was not only customary, it was also very sensible.

Farmyard play continues with this pig-tailed girl. She (her name is Jean) is wearing a similarly sashed pinafore over her red dress. This image is from a reading textbook appropriately titled *At Play*.

A pig-tailed girl named Jean wearing a pinafore style apron at the farm. *At Play*, page 29, ©The John C. Winston Company, 1940.

If you're looking for directions for making cocoa, you might visit the kitchen of these young girls. Ingredients and utensils at the ready, all three are wearing their aprons. Each has slightly different detailing. Look closely for rickrack edging, button closures, collars, calico fabric, decorative embroidery, and sashes. If you want to join them, you'll want an apron, too. You won't need to bring cooking supplies. They're all there—even the timer and the tea kettle.

Three young girls in aprons, busy in the kitchen, preparing cocoa. *Day by Day*, page 47, ©Allyn and Bacon, 1939.

Among the more endearing scenes of children helping Mom in the kitchen is this rendition from the 1930 *Elson-Gray Basic Reader.* Mother sports a half apron with an oversize sash and bow. Each of the children is draped in one of mother's aprons, each hitched up around the neck and tied in a bow. The boy in the foreground has his apron sashes draped over the shoulders, across the back, and returned to the front in a bow. Making and baking cutout cookies are the main activity.

Portrayals of children in the kitchen with an *aproned grandmother* are common. Pictured in the 1946 General Mills children's book, *Eat and Grow,* a young girl in suspendered play clothes assists her gray-haired grand-mother with the drying of the dishes. Grandmother's half apron suggests a gingham checked or plaid style with a hefty bow.

An aproned woman washing dishes (with drying assistance from a little girl). The suggested style is a gingham half apron. *Eat and Grow,* ©General Mills, Inc., 1946.

Woman (in her half apron) and three children (in oversize aprons hitched up around the neck) making and baking cutout cookies. *Elson-Gray Basic Reader,* page 27, ©Scott, Foresman and Company, 1930 and 1936.

The tradition of women and girls in the kitchen is evident in many patterns and publications of the mid-twentieth century. Cookbooks, textbooks, and children's storybooks abound with illustrations and pictures of women and girls outfitted in aprons. Often they are in coordinating styles.

A woman and girl appear in matching bright red gingham aprons on the cover of The Proctor & Gamble Company's *Recipes for Good Eating* (1945). Each apron has a full frontal bib, generous shoulder ruffles, and huge pockets. Red checks and gingerbread cutout cookies never looked better.

In *Some of My Favorite Good Things to Eat* (1940), the experts at Arm & Hammer picture an entourage of a woman and a child (and the cat) proudly displaying their glazed and frosted layer cakes. The woman's apron is a full length bibbed, sashed, and fancy style—complete with ornamented twin pockets. The girl's apron is also bibbed, sashed, and decorated with a ruffle. Both appear to be heading straight from the kitchen to the dining room, properly attired and in anticipation of a happy celebration.

The woman and girl on the cover of *Home Baking Made Easy for Beginners and Experts* (Lever Brothers Company, 1953) have matching aprons. That's not all. They also have matching dresses and mixing bowls. Sunny yellow fabric, bright red trim, and shoulder ruffles are the main ingredients of the aprons. *Spry* is the main ingredient of whatever it is they are concocting.

Women and girls made their way into the home economics textbooks, too. This aproned pair is serving up garden salads and fresh buttermilk biscuits on page 68 of the book, *How You Plan and Prepare Meals*. Stripes, checks, and plain cloth were all included in the making of these aprons. Details include bibs, around-the-neck shoulder straps, and huge pockets.

TOP TO BOTTOM:
Woman and girl in matching bright red gingham aprons. *Recipes for Good Eating*, ©The Proctor and Gamble Company, 1945.

Woman and girl in full length bibbed, sashed, ruffled, fancy style aprons. *Some of My Favorite Good Things to Eat*, ©Church & Dwight Co., Inc., 1940.

Woman and girl with matching aprons, matching dresses, and matching mixing bowls. *Home Baking Made Easy for Beginners and Experts*, ©Lever Brothers Company, 1953.

Matching plaid bibbed aprons are the choice of this woman and girl for serving up salad and fresh buttermilk biscuits. *How You Plan and Prepare Meals*, page 68, ©McGraw-Hill Book Company, 1962 and 1968.

High School Home Economics

Textbooks for junior and senior high school home economics students in the 1950s and 60s were strewn with apron-clad students, both female and male. Page 22 of the 1956 textbook *Experiences with Foods* pictures four students (two boys and two girls) gathered around a kitchen table, enjoying a snack of sandwiches, fruit, and milk. One girl is outfitted in a bibbed and sashed white apron. One of the boys is wearing a gathered and sashed green apron. All appear to be enjoying themselves.

Throughout the texts, girls and boys alike are shown in illustrations of food preparation and kitchen management. An over-the-shoulder apron, a large mixing bowl, and a one-quart liquid measure are some of the requirements for the girl pictured here. The text admonishes:

> Whatever the meal you are preparing, there are two basic requirements to keep in mind—cleanliness and safety. Cleanliness is absolutely essential in the kitchen. Before beginning your work, make careful personal preparation. You should wear a dress or apron made from washable material. Bib aprons, wide at the side, afford the best protection.

An over-the-shoulder apron, a large mixing bowl, and a one quart liquid measure are some of the kitchen requirements for this young woman. *Experiences with Foods,* page 25, ©Ginn and Company, 1956.

Boys and girls in a high school home economics classroom. One of the boys is wearing a gathered and sashed green apron. One girl is outfitted in a bibbed and sashed white apron. *Experiences with Foods,* page 22, ©Ginn and Company, 1956.

Girls in both bibbed and cobbler style aprons are carefully filing recipes and washing and drying dishes in this home economics kitchen. It's clear that they have read the suggestions in Chapter 27 of the 1962 textbook *How You Plan And Prepare Meals:*

At school as well as at home, you should protect your clothing by wearing an apron. Your apron should . . .

. . . be one which you enjoy wearing—not 'just any old thing.'

. . . be becoming in color and be made of a material that launders easily.

. . . be made in a pleasing style which protects most of your dress.

. . . fit properly, look neat, and be easy to put on and remove.

. . . have pockets large enough for your handkerchief, and so on.

According to the same textbook:

Boys usually wear large butcher aprons to protect their clothing. Most boys roll up their shirt sleeves while working in the kitchen to keep their cuffs from becoming soiled.

And here's proof—the table is properly set, the food ready to be served, and the hosts are well protected with full length bibbed aprons.

The white puffed sleeve blouse of this young lady will be well protected with this stylish bibbed and collared apron. The novelty printed apron fabric is carefully decorated and edged with rickrack. Bacon and eggs are on the menu, and the cook's outfit will be safeguarded from spatters or spills.

And which apron would you select for readying a pan of ring bologna for the oven? A handmade gingham apron is the choice of this young cook. Design details include 1/4 inch checks, sashing, and generous amounts of hand smocking along the upper edge. Do you think she made it in her high school home economics class? Or did she raid her mother's kitchen drawer?

TOP TO BOTTOM:
Young women in bibbed and cobbler style aprons carefully filing recipes and washing and drying dishes in a home economics kitchen. *How You Plan and Prepare Meals,* page 389, ©McGraw-Hill Book Company, 1962 and 1968.

The table is properly set, the food ready to be served, and the hosts are well protected with full length bibbed aprons. *How You Plan and Prepare Meals,* page 410.

This novelty print fabric apron is carefully decorated and edged with rickrack. Bacon and eggs are on the menu, and the cook's outfit will be safeguarded from spatters or spills. *How You Plan and Prepare Meals,* page 413.

A handmade gingham apron is the choice of this young cook. Design details include 1/4 inch checks, sashing, and hand smocking. *How You Plan and Prepare Meals,* page 108.

Queen of the Kitchen

During the 1930s, 40s, 50s, and 60s, editors and illustrators of magazines often portrayed women in a stereotypical housewife role. Here's an American Gas Association advertisement from the March 1945 *Better Homes and Gardens* magazine. One illustration shows a bedraggled woman with her hair tied atop her head, a broom in her hands, and a pile of dirty dishes heaped on the table. She is wearing a bibbed and sashed white apron. The children appear to be looking admiringly at her. (Just why *they* aren't doing the dishes, I don't know.) The illustration is labeled 'Your Problem'. The caption reads:

> You want a new kitchen. A better kitchen. Where everything really works together to save you steps, time, energy. A cool, clean, beautiful place—where you can spend fifteen hundred hours a year and like it!

The prominent accompanying illustration shows the 'new freedom gas kitchen.' A transformation has taken place. The housewife is now smartly coiffed and more stylishly attired. However, she is still wearing the bibbed and sashed white apron. The illustration is labeled:

> New freedom . . . new convenience for *every* woman who cooks.

I think a *"Honey, I'm home!"* caption would be more appropriate.

An advertisement for the American Gas Company from the March 1945 *Better Homes and Gardens* magazine. The bedraggled woman is wearing a bibbed and sashed white apron. ©American Gas Company and Meredith Corporation, 1945.

The same magazine and the same woman, now smartly coiffed and more stylishly attired with a clean white apron. The illustration is labeled *"New freedom . . new convenience for every woman who cooks."* Perhaps a *"Honey, I'm Home!"* caption would be more appropriate. ©American Gas Company and Meredith Corporation, 1945.

Aproned women grace the covers of a myriad of cookbooks—carrying everything from fresh eggs to lavishly decorated layer cakes. Apron protection is suggested for everything from peeling apples and making preserves to frying eggs and setting the table to mixing the cake batter and baking a pie.

Could there be a more welcoming and gracious appearing woman than the beaming brunette from the 1945 *Baking is Fun. . . The Ann Pillsbury Way* cookbook? You can't help but like her smiling disposition, her stylish hairdo, her decorated cake, and her ruffled and pocketed gingham apron. The cover of the cookbook pictures the same woman in the early stages of cake preparation, with a mixing bowl, measuring cups, and ingredients within easy reach.

Aprons also figure significantly in the 1951 General Foods Corporation booklet *What Makes Jelly "Jell"?* The woman concocting the orange marmalade in Lesson 4 wears a protective bibbed apron with wide shoulder straps and a collar. During the preparation of her strawberry preserves, she is outfitted with a bibbed gingham apron. Trimmed with bias edging, the checked apron makes a rather jarring contrast with her striped cotton dress.

TOP TO BOTTOM:

A gracious and welcoming woman in her ruffled and pocketed gingham apron. *Baking is Fun. . . The Ann Pillsbury Way*, ©Pillsbury Mills, Inc., 1945.

The cover of the cookbook pictures the same aproned woman in the early stages of cake preparation—a mixing bowl, measuring cups, and ingredients within easy reach. *Baking is Fun. . . The Ann Pillsbury Way*, 1945.

A woman wears a protective bibbed apron with wide shoulder straps and a collar while preparing her orange marmalade. *What Makes Jelly "Jell"?*, page 18, ©General Foods Corporation, 1951.

During the preparation of her strawberry preserves, this woman is outfitted with a bibbed gingham apron. *What Makes Jelly "Jell"?*, page 20, ©General Foods Corporation, 1951.

Rickrack edging is the decoration of choice for the young woman preparing the morning's fried eggs. Her pink gathered apron is edged with white rickrack. Pictured in a 1955 *Little Golden Book*, this over-the-shoulder bibbed style apron was both popular and practical.

A giant bow and generous ruffles highlight this redhead's apron. The gently rounded, form-fitting style is quite becoming for a woman ready to serve her family or guests. The table is properly set, including linens and dinnerware, and the hostess looks quite fetching in her polka dot apron, water pitcher at the ready.

This young woman's pink bibbed and gathered apron is edged with white rickrack. *Numbers - A Little Golden Book*, ©Simon and Schuster, 1955.

A gently rounded, form fitting style is quite becoming for this woman. Apron details include a giant bow and generous ruffles. *Day by Day*, ©Allyn and Bacon, 1939.

Cookbooks published in the 1940s emphasized the economy of war-time. In the 1943 cookbook *300 Helpful Suggestions for Your Victory Lunch Box* families are pictured in cheerful and cooperative efforts preparing and serving food for less expense and at a reduced energy output. The woman pictured here is consulting her list of 300 suggestions. (The booklet was designed to hang conveniently from the cupboard's edge at eye level.) And of course, she is wearing an apron—a bibbed and pocketed style that goes over the shoulder and around the neck.

The woman pictured here is consulting her list of 300 suggestions. She is wearing a bibbed and pocketed apron that goes over the shoulder and around the neck. *300 Helpful Suggestions for Your Victory Lunch Box*, ©Dell Publishing Co., Inc., 1943.

Good Things to Eat

MADE WITH

ARM & HAMMER BAKING SODA

107th EDITION

The 1933 booklet *Good Things to Eat Made with Arm & Hammer Baking Soda* features a rather somber young woman on the cover. Her blue, yellow, and white chemise-style apron amply covers her dark blue dress. The large plaid fabric used in the apron is a type of gingham. Supplied with fresh fruit, milk, a giant mixing bowl that matches her apron, teakettle, sugar bowl, pitcher, and the all-important ingredient—baking soda—she is on her way to preparation of some 'good things to eat'.

Even more captivating is the smiling fair-haired maiden on the cover of *The New Dr. Price Cook Book (for use with Dr. Price's Phosphate Baking Powder)*. She prefers baking powder to baking soda. Instead of a 'full' bibbed apron she favors an extra long gingham checkered 'half' apron, which is hitched up high above the waistline for added protection and tied in the back. The filled and frosted layer cake and her appearance and demeanor suggest equal skills at cooking and coquetry.

Gardening, Gathering, and Storekeeping

A generously cut plain white apron is a sensible choice for the woman pictured in the 1938 *Down the River Road* reading text-book. Her bright red dress and lap are amply protected while she peels and cores apples for a pie. Simply cut from plain material, this no-frills apron style was suitable for all sorts of household tasks. *She* is seated in a straight back chair while she works (sugar, canister and scoop, mixing bowl, and measuring cup on the nearby table). *He* is relaxing with a beverage in the comfortable rocking chair.

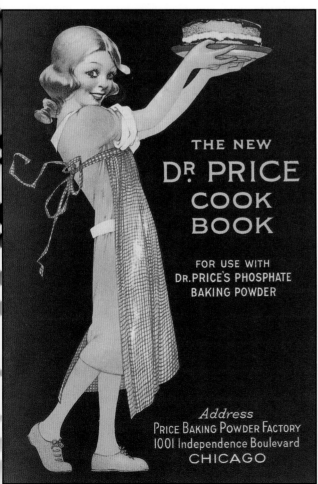

THE NEW

DR. PRICE COOK BOOK

FOR USE WITH
DR. PRICE'S PHOSPHATE
BAKING POWDER

Address
PRICE BAKING POWDER FACTORY
1001 Independence Boulevard
CHICAGO

A generously cut plain white apron is a sensible choice for a woman while she peels apples for a pie. *Down the River Road*, page 67, ©Row, Peterson and Company, 1938.

TOP LEFT, BOTTOM LEFT:
This somber young woman favors a blue, yellow, and white chemise-style plaid apron. *Good Things to Eat Made with Arm & Hammer Baking Soda*, ©Church & Dwight Co., Inc., 1933.

An extra long gingham checkered half apron provides protection for this smiling fair-haired maiden. *The New Dr. Price Cook Book*, ©Royal Baking Powder Co., 1921.

And now the pie is ready for the oven. *She* still looks fresh and protected in her red dress and white apron. *He* remains seated with folded hands in the comfortable rocking chair, admiring the progress of the aproned woman.

You can practically smell the aroma of fresh baked bread from the old-fashioned wood cook stove in this scene. Grandmother is attired in a long sleeved blue dress and a bright red floor-length apron. Taken from the pages of the 1939 Alice and Jerry reading textbook *Through the Green Gate*, the illustration includes a vivid red and white checkered tablecloth, a towel drying rack, a bucket of coal, and a hand water pump in the background.

Excitement reigns in another scene of a grandmother and a trio of boys in shorts and knickers. Gardening and berry picking are the activities. Bearing both a basket and a bucket of berries, the boys have returned to their grandmother, who pauses to wipe her hands on her long red gathered apron and admire their produce.

Moving from the kitchen to the garden to the chicken coop, we find this elderly woman and young boy gathering freshly laid eggs. Grannie's pink apron requires yards of fabric—it's extra long and thickly gathered, and the sashes are particularly wide. Yes, it provides ample protection for her fairly fancy outfit. And it would also be suitable for the wiping of hands and the transporting of gathered eggs.

And finally, a man wearing an apron—in the typical behind-the-counter storekeeper role. We get a rear view glimpse of the man in his rolled up sleeves and butcher-style apron: Durable plain white cloth, cut wide and long to reach around the sides and below the knees, a thin strap around the neck, and narrow ties at the back. Is that a loaf of fresh bread he's wrapping in brown paper for the little girl?

TOP: Grandmother is attired in a long sleeved blue dress and a bright red floor-length apron. *Through the Green Gate*, page 49, ©Row, Peterson and Company, 1939.
BOTTOM: Gardening and berry picking are the main activities here. And grandmother pauses to wipe her hands on her long red gathered apron and admire the produce. *Through the Green Gate*, page 12.

The pie is ready for the oven and the woman still looks fresh and protected in her red dress and white apron. *Down the River Road*, page 68.

TOP: Moving from the kitchen to the chicken coop, we find an elderly woman in a pink apron. Extra long and thickly gathered, it might be suitable for gathering eggs. *Elson-Gray Basic Readers, Book One*, ©Scott, Foresman, and Company, 1930 and 1936.
BOTTOM: And finally, a man wearing a butcher-style apron made from durable plain white cloth, cut wide and long, with thin straps and narrow ties. *Elson-Gray Basic Readers, Book One*.

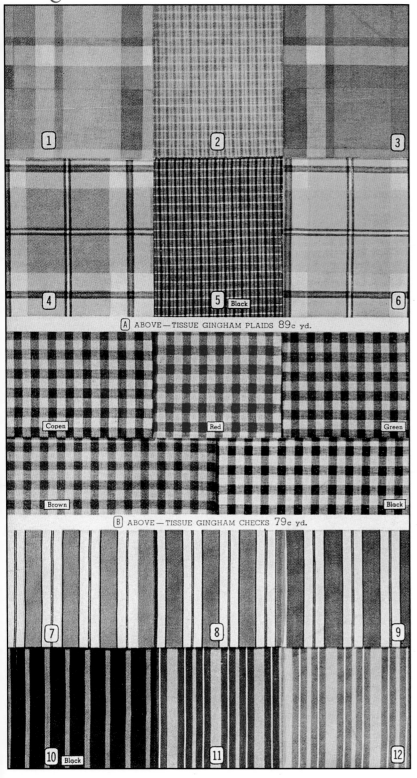

A ABOVE—TISSUE GINGHAM PLAIDS 89¢ yd.

B ABOVE—TISSUE GINGHAM CHECKS 79¢ yd.

A Checkered Past

A study of the major mail order catalogs of the past century reveals the assorted gingham fabrics available for home sewing. Sears, Roebuck and Co. and Montgomery Ward catalogs picture a wide selection of checkered cloth in varying widths and colors.

The term 'gingham' is a modification of the Malay *genggang*, meaning checkered cloth. It is defined as 'a clothing fabric usually of yarn-dyed cotton in plain weave'. Another source further describes gingham as 'from the Malay *gingan*, a cotton cloth, usually in stripes or checks, or two or more colors, woven of dyed yarn, and used for dresses, aprons, etc.'

In the earlier catalogs of the 1920s and 30s, the word gingham is applied more generally to include not only checkered cloth (one color plus white) but also plaid fabrics (two or more colors), and occasionally striped cloth. The illustration from the 1953 Montgomery Ward Spring/Summer catalog groups all three—plaids, checks, and stripes—on the same page. All are labeled 'gingham.' The plaid samples have two or three colors. The checks are one color against white. The stripes are dual and multi-colored. The description on page 222 reads:

> Ameritex tissue gingham checks in bright colors contrasted with white. Sheer, comfortable. Permanent crease-resistant finish. Combed, preshrunk cotton, max. shrinkage 3%. Extra wide 43 inches in 5 washfast, sunfast colors, shown 1/2 size. 79¢ yd.

The illustration from this catalog groups plaids, checks, and stripes on the same page. All are labeled 'gingham'. *1953 Spring/Summer Montgomery Ward Catalog*, page 222, ©Montgomery Ward.

Another listing on page 224 of the same catalog groups and labels both plaids and checks as 'yardstick' ginghams:

Galey & Lord 'Yardstick' Ginghams. . . You're getting one of the finest Ginghams made when you buy Galey & Lord's 'Yardstick' Gingham. Selected by leading designers for distinctive casual fashion, there's top quality and high-styling in every yard. Woven of long-staple combed cotton for smoother, finer texture. Sanforized, crease-resistant, colors are sunfast, vat dyed and washfast. Width 35 inches, 87¢ yd.

A more detailed selection is shown in the 1956-57 Montgomery Ward Fall/Winter catalog:

Burlington's crease-resistant Gingham. You'll be smart to choose checks for the bright spot in your wardrobe. Fine combed cotton; crease-resistant finish assures better appearance and easier laundering. For at-home frocks, blouses and family play clothes . . . 1/4 and 1/8 inch checks in 9 colors. Sunfast, washfast. Max. shrinkage 1%, 35 in. wide, 69¢ yd.

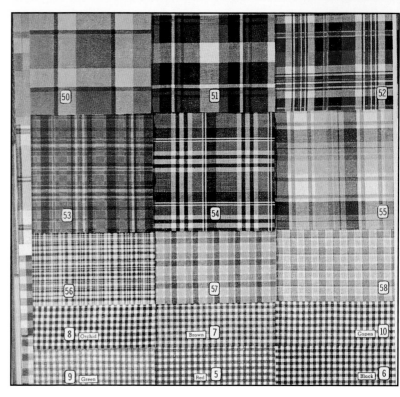

Fine and classic ginghams available in six colors (orchid, brown, copen, green, red, and black) for 87¢ per yard. *1953 Spring/Summer Montgomery Ward Catalog, page 224,* ©Montgomery Ward.

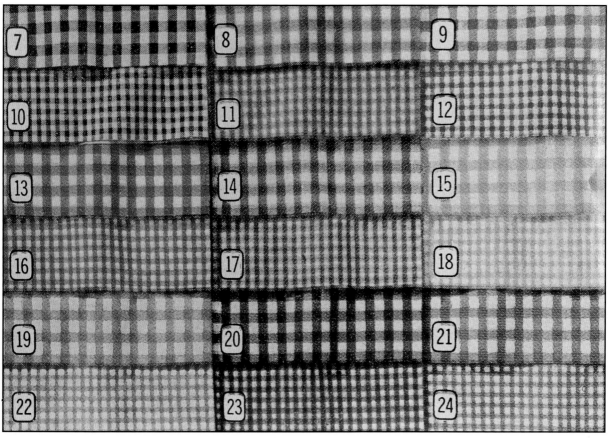

Gingham in two sizes (1/8 inch and 1/4 inch) and nine colors (black, green, red, turquoise, brown, blue, pink, navy, and orchid) for 69¢ per yard. *1956/57 Fall/Winter Montgomery Ward Catalog, page 258,* ©Montgomery Ward.

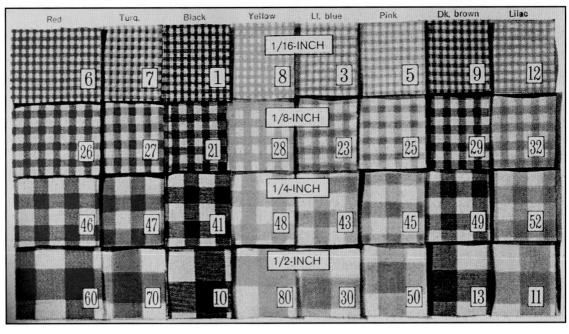

Dan River Cotton Gingham in four sizes (1/16 inch, 1/8 inch, 1/4 inch, and 1/2 inch) and eight colors (red, turquoise, black, yellow, light blue, pink, dark brown, and lilac) at 64¢ per yard. *1964 Fall/Winter Sears Catalog*, page 377, ©Sears, Roebuck and Co.

Extremely narrow and exceedingly wide checks are less commonly found. The real eye-catchers, if only for their rarity, are 1/16 inch, 1/2 inch, and 1 inch wide gingham. The tiny checks allow for wee cross stitches and fine embellishments. The wider checks offer large spaces and lend a sense of drama. Several good examples of both narrow and wide ginghams are included in the book.

The 1964 Fall and Winter Sears catalog includes all five sizes of gingham. The 1/16 inch, 1/8 inch, 1/4 inch, and 1/2 inch widths are grouped together on page 377. At sixty-four cents a yard, the Dan River fabric is described as:

Yarn-dyed checks . . . color is woven in, not just printed on. Wrinkl-Shed® with Dri-Don. All combed cotton. Machine wash and wear (hot temperature). Maximum shrinkage 1%. Minimum iron. Needs no starch. 36 inches wide.

The eight available colors included red, turquoise, black, yellow, light blue, pink, dark brown, and lilac.

The one inch wide woven checks are pictured on the following page of the catalog. These, too, were available in eight colors. Also priced at sixty-four cents a yard, the description is similar, but adds:

Tablecloth checks . . . their popularity now spreads to curtains, quilts, smocked decorator pillow covers, leisure wear, shifts.

One inch wide woven Dan River Gingham, also available in eight colors at 64¢ per yard. *1964 Fall/Winter Sears Catalog*, page 378, ©Sears, Roebuck and Co.

A graphic arrangement of the different sizes of checks is made in the accompanying illustration. Five colors and sizes are shown: 1 inch blue, 1/2 inch green, 1/4 inch red, 1/8 inch yellow, and 1/16 inch turquoise. Each sample strip of fabric is two inches wide, for easier visual comparison.

An arrangement of red checkered cloth in the five widths is also shown. Again, a two inch width of each fabric is revealed for accurate visual comparison. The 1 inch check reveals two rows of checks, the 1/2 inch check reveals four rows of checks, the 1/4 inch check reveals eight rows of checks, the 1/8 inch check reveals sixteen rows of checks, and the 1/16 inch cloth reveals thirty-two rows of checks.

A more appealing illustration pictures the actual sash ends from five lipstick red aprons, one example for each of the five check widths. A twelve inch ruler serves as a guide to compare the dimensions of the checks and sashes, which range from two to three inches wide.

The most available (and hence most popular) check widths were 1/8 inch and 1/4 inch. More than ninety percent of the aprons in this book are made from 1/8 inch or 1/4 inch gingham fabric. These widths are very suitable for cross stitched designs. They are also appropriate for rickrack decoration.

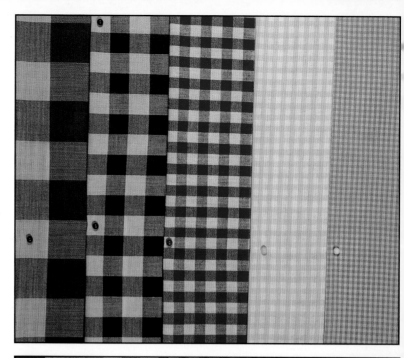

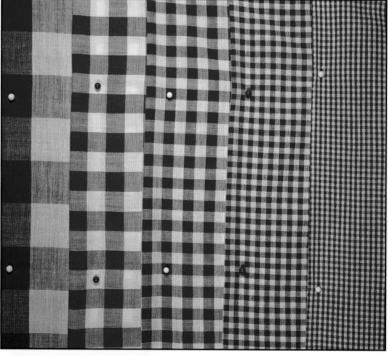

Five widths and five colors of gingham: 1 inch blue, 1/2 inch green, 1/4 inch red, 1/8 inch yellow, and 1/16 inch turquoise. For accurate comparison, a two inch width of each fabric is revealed.

An arrangement of red checkered cloth in five widths. A two inch width of each fabric is revealed.

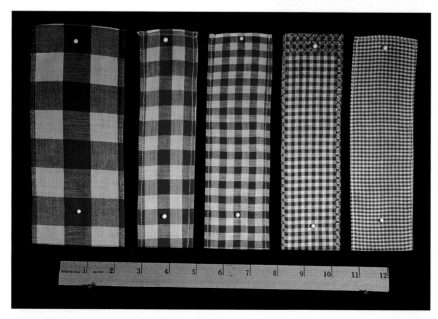

Sash ends from five red aprons, one example for each of the five widths. A twelve inch ruler serves as a guide to compare the dimensions of the checks and sashes.

The two small needlework projects shown here illustrate the adaptability of 1/8 inch checks. The paired potholders are trimmed with regular size silver and white rickrack. The rounded edges are bound with white bias trim. The cross stitched holiday stocking is also made with 1/8 inch gingham. Red and white double cross stitches lend a luminous quality to the fabric.

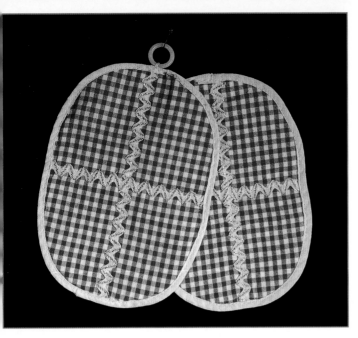

Paired potholders made from 1/8 inch red gingham, trimmed with regular size silver and white rickrack, and bound with white bias trim.

A cross stitched holiday stocking made with 1/8 inch gingham. Red and white double cross stitches lend a luminous quality to the fabric.

I found this colorful array of 1/4 inch gingham fabric in a resale shop—materials obviously selected for one woman's apron projects. One-yard lengths of cotton fabric in red, yellow, lavender, blue, and pink are ready to be cut and assembled into aprons. The pointed sashes for the pink apron have been cut and sewn. Nothing else has been completed, so there is plenty of work yet to be done.

A colorful array of 1/4 inch gingham fabric—one yard lengths in red, yellow, lavender, blue, and pink—ready to be cut and assembled into aprons.

Printed Patterns

During my initial research on aprons, I collected dozens of printed patterns. Many of these are shown in my first book about aprons, *Aprons of the Mid-20th Century: To Serve and Protect*. More than twenty-five vintage apron printed patterns are pictured, including childrens' aprons, half aprons, bibbed aprons, smocks, cobbler aprons, and mother/daughter combination patterns. Some apron pattern kits are also pictured. Some of those patterns were appropriate for gingham fabrics, and a few included checked fabrics in their 'suggested' fabric renditions.

Many needlework pattern companies produced cross stitch designs for gingham aprons. *Simplicity printed pattern #4726* contains a collection of designs described as '*8 full color charts of 13 motifs or border designs for cross stitch embroidery on 1/8-inch check gingham.*' Included are roses, daisies, poinsettias, paper doll cutouts, butterflies, hearts, chickens, fish, geometric shapes, and a sailor.

Another example of a commercially printed pattern—*McCall's #6664*—pictures two smocked aprons, one bibbed, one half. The pattern envelope reads '*junior and misses' checked gingham smocked aprons.*' For more pictures and styles of smocked aprons, check out the 'Smocking' section of this book, which includes eight additional styles and colors.

Vogart Transfer Pattern #127 contains a variety of cross stitched designs suitable for kitchen and assorted household linens, including aprons. The young woman on the pattern envelope is drying dishes with a freshly cross stitched dish towel. (Why is she using the 'glasses' towel to wipe the plates?) More importantly, she is wearing a handsome deep forest green gingham apron—gathered, bibbed, and sashed.

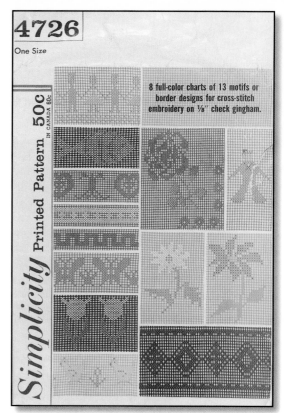

Simplicity Printed Pattern #4726 contains a collection of '8 full color charts of 13 motifs or border designs for cross stitch embroidery on 1/8 inch check gingham.' ©Simplicity Pattern Co., Inc.

McCall's Printed Pattern #6664 featuring two styles of smocked aprons in junior and misses' sizes, suitable for gingham fabric. ©McCall Corporation. Courtesy of Dorothy Gilbertson.

Vogart Transfer Pattern #127 contains a variety of cross stitched designs suitable for kitchen and assorted household linens, including aprons. The woman pictured here is wearing a handsome deep forest green gingham apron—gathered, bibbed, and sashed. ©Vogart Co., Inc.

Many transfer and cross stitch patterns included designs appropriate for aprons. Some pictured whimsical and carefree maidens in decorative aprons. *Aunt Martha's Studios* published many designs appropriate for gingham checks such as the flowers, bows, and streamers shown here. Each package included a complete design chart and set of instructions.

Used transfer pattern of young maiden with apron decorated with cross stitches. *Courtesy of Pat Schoen.*

Aunt Martha's Cross Stitch Design #3561 for gingham checks, with complete chart and instructions for bow and streamers. ©Aunt Martha's Studios. *Courtesy of Betty Wilson.*

Aunt Martha's Cross Stitch Design #3558 for gingham checks, with complete chart and instructions for a large daisy design. ©Aunt Martha's Studios. *Courtesy of Betty Wilson.*

One of my treasured apron patterns is labeled number 5014 *Gingham Aprons with Cross-Stitch Borders*. It lists the materials needed, directions, and illustrations for a gathered and sashed half apron. Two design options for a 'rose border' and a 'star flower border' are included. It is printed in black and white, with no credit for the publishing company or copyright listed on the pattern sheet. (Perhaps it was a mail order pattern.) It gives just the basics needed to complete a traditional half apron—the style of the majority of the aprons pictured in this book. With just a touch of ingenuity, most seamstresses could adapt these elementary instructions to create an apron with their own personal touch. Others with years of home sewing experience wouldn't even need these basic instructions.

Pattern 5014, Gingham Aprons with Cross-Stitch Borders (publisher unknown) lists materials needed, directions, and illustrations for a gathered and sashed half apron.

Two cross stitch design options for a 'rose border' and a 'star flower border' are included with *Pattern 5014*.

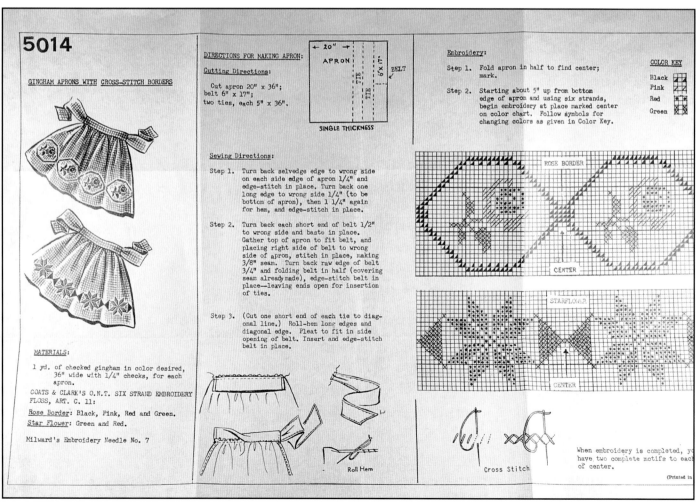

I have selected eight works-in-progress (unfinished or abandoned projects, really) to illustrate the steps for making a gingham apron. These are all needlework projects that I found in garage sales, second hand stores, or my mother's closet.

Several include only the skirt portion of the apron, with varying degrees of progress on a hand cross stitched design. Some still have the threaded needle inserted in the cloth. Other examples show the apron near completion, with details such as sashing or decorative stitching to be completed.

Ordinarily, the first step in construction of a cross stitched gingham apron would be to cut a large panel of material for the skirt. This was usually cut the width of the fabric (thirty-six inches in most aprons from the mid-twentieth century, forty-five inches in more recent times) and anywhere from eighteen to thirty inches deep, depending on the preferred length of the skirt and depth of the hem. The next step would be to do the cross stitching. The design could be marked lightly on the fabric. Or you could simply count the checks as you stitched.

The first example shows a 1/8 inch turquoise gingham panel with the beginnings of a border design. Using triple stranded black embroidery floss, the first half of each cross stitch (a diagonal stitch) has been carefully worked on the white squares. The second half of each cross stitch (a diagonal stitch in the opposite direction) is being added.

A 1/8 inch turquoise gingham panel with the beginnings of a border design using triple stranded black embroidery floss.

The first half of each cross stitch (a diagonal stitch) has been carefully worked on the white squares. The second half of each cross stitch (a diagonal stitch in the opposite direction) is being added.

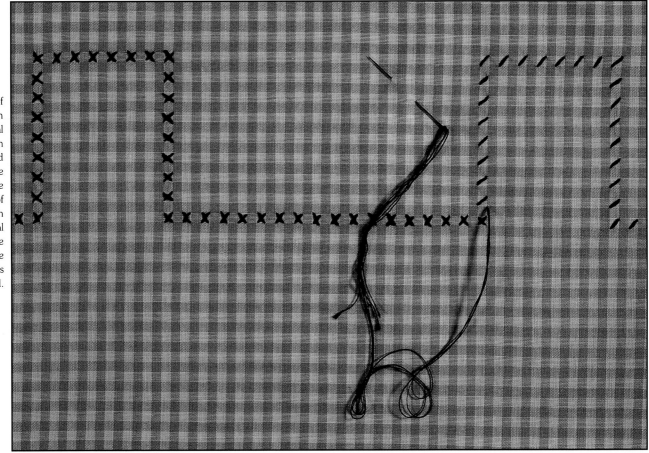

The second example is a
1/8 inch lavender checked
fabric. The skirt panel has a
two inch wide rectangular
border design of mixed
'crossed' and 'uncrossed'
stitches. Two colors of embroidery floss are being used.
Large purple uncrossed stitches
placed on white squares make
up the central portion of the
design. Rows of tiny black X's
frame the upper and lower
edges of the pattern.

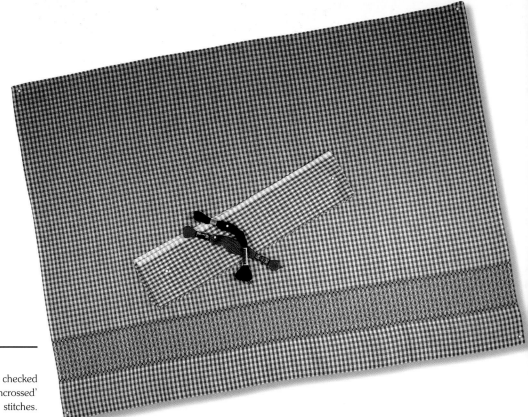

An apron skirt panel of 1/8 inch lavender checked
fabric with mixed 'crossed' and 'uncrossed'
stitches.

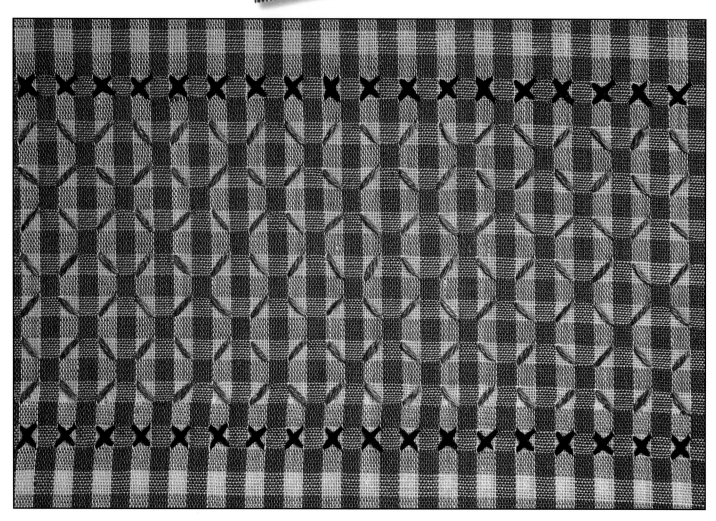

Two colors of embroidery floss are being used. Large purple uncrossed stitches placed on white squares
make up the central portion of the design. Rows of tiny black X's frame the upper and lower edges.

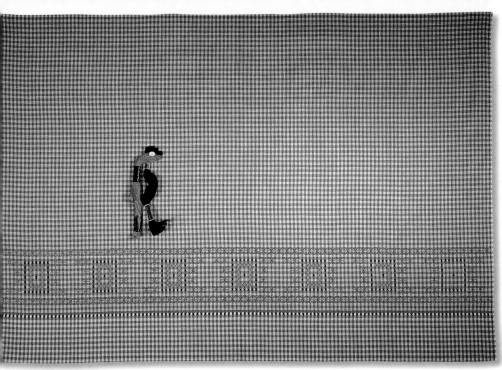

The third example shows a more elaborate border pattern in various stages of completion. Turquoise and black embroidery floss are used for the cross stitches. Large aqua double cross stitches make up the major portion of the design. Tiny stitches in both colors accent and complete each inner design.

An elaborate border pattern in various stages of completion. Turquoise and black embroidery floss are used for the cross stitches.

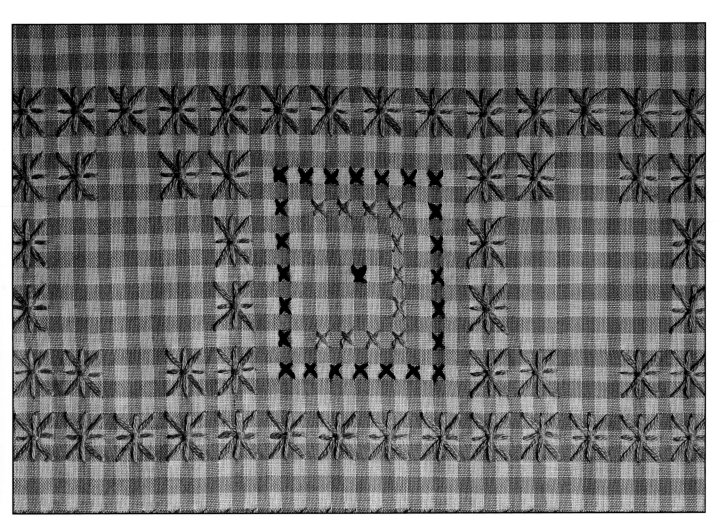

Large turquoise double cross stitches make up the major portion of the design.
Tiny stitches in both colors accent and complete each inner design.

The beginnings of acorns and oak leaves appear on the next example. Using a light green gingham for the background, colorful leaves are being stitched along the lower edge of the skirt panel. Decorative acorns with dark brown caps and stems are stitched across the waistband piece.

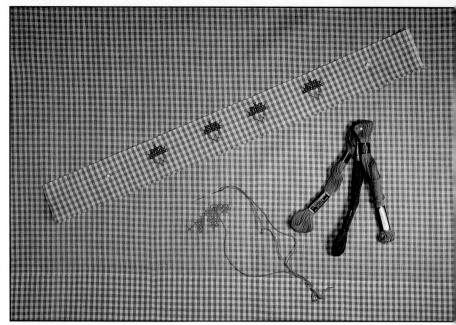

The beginnings of oak leaves appear on this light green gingham apron panel.

Decorative acorns with dark brown caps and stems are stitched across the waistband piece.

A caramel-colored panel of 1/4 inch gingham serves as the background for this intricate border design. Stitching is done with yellow and white embroidery floss. Yellow cross stitches are placed on the white squares, giving a feeling of darkness to the lower edge of the design. White cross stitches are placed on the yellow squares, giving a feeling of lightness to the center designs. Choice of thread and placement of stitches make all the difference in the impact of this design.

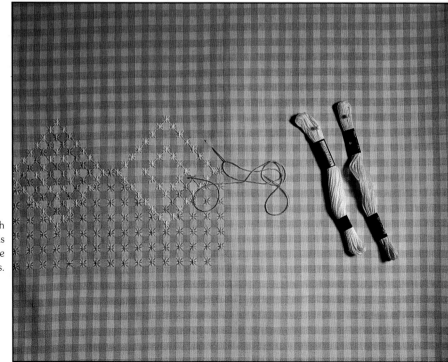

A caramel-colored panel of 1/4 inch gingham serves as the background for this intricate border design. Stitching is done with yellow and white embroidery floss.

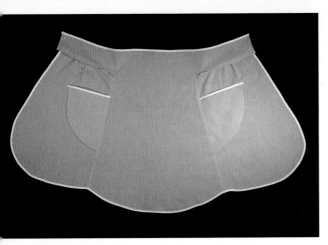

A distinctively shaped apron using 1/16 inch aqua gingham. The main skirt panel is gently rounded and has side inserts which are lightly gathered at the top.

This distinctively shaped apron with its gently rounded edges is constructed from 1/16 inch aqua gingham. The main skirt panel has side inserts that are lightly gathered at the top. The odd shaped three-sided pockets are bound with white bias along the top and inserted into the seams. Work yet to be done includes hand application of the pocket edges, final stitching of the white trim around the apron, and addition of the sashes.

What's missing on this orange 'work-in-progress'? Construction of the apron is essentially complete—skirt hem, side hems, pocket, waistband, and sashes. On first inspection, I thought this was a finished, albeit undecorated, apron. On closer inspection, I found faint markings for a cross stitched design along the lower edge. Barely visible diagonal hash marks are scattered across the skirt. The handwork was never completed. But the apron is still usable in its unadorned state.

An orange 'work-in-progress' with completed construction, but missing the cross stitching.

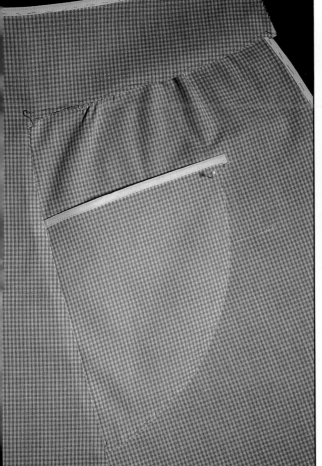

The odd shaped three-sided pockets are bound with white bias along the top and inserted into the seams.

Barely visible markings for a cross stitched design are scattered along the lower edge of the apron. Look for faint diagonal marks.

The final example leaves me baffled. What's confusing are the little black cross stitch markings across the apron and along the waistband. Didn't we all just assume that thread was one of the requirements for making a cross stitched apron? Not so for this pea soup green checked apron, which has a five-star design marked on the skirt. These appear to be done with an ink marker, perhaps indelibly. Were they marked before the apron was constructed? Are they the marked patterns for yet-to-be-done hand cross stitching? Are they intended to be the final pattern, a cross stitched design in ink instead of thread? Perhaps this is a store bought apron or pattern from a kit. The apron has several of the markings of a factory made apron—surged edges, crooked seams, machine binding, dangling threads, and inferior workmanship.

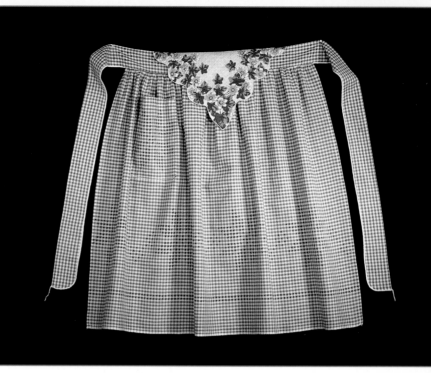

A pea soup green checked apron with a five-star design marked on the skirt. These appear to be done with an ink marker, perhaps indelibly.

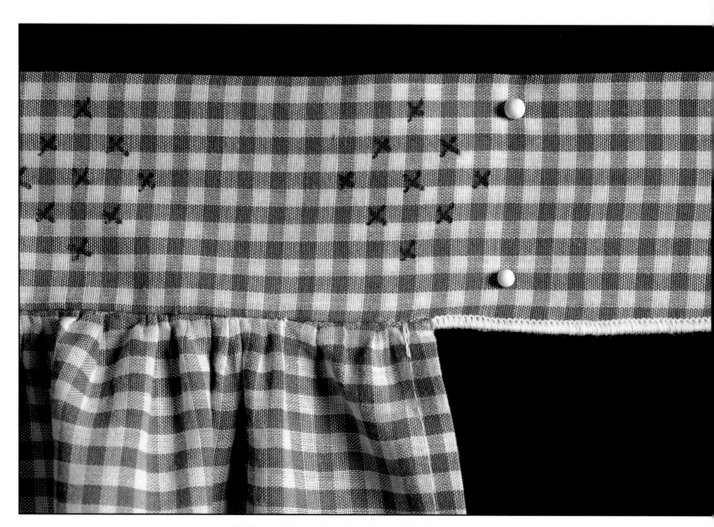

Evidence of ink markings along the waistband, crooked gathers, and machine surged edges along the sashes.

Section One:
Cross Stitch

The gallery of gingham aprons is organized into three major sections based on types of decoration, design techniques, and fabric styles. The first section includes aprons with cross stitched designs, which is the most common gingham apron style. This is the checkered style most people recall being worn by their mothers and grandmothers.

The cross stitched designs are further subdivided by border styles, patterns, and types of stitching. The first section covers what I have described as **Basic Borders,** i.e., plain and simple rectangular panels, with little adornment and variation. They range from extremely narrow to very wide and in a colorful array of threads and fabrics. These aprons may appear ordinary, but some are far from it. One red and white checkered number has more than 2,345 little red X's!

The second section features more elaborate borders, some with diamonds, triangles, squares—hence the label **Geometric Borders**. These borders include shapes and designs that are more elaborate than the rectangular patterns. Some might even call them fancy! Portions of these 'fancy' border designs often appear on the pockets, as well.

Twelve aprons with cross stitched star designs comprise the third section, titled **A Stellar Display**. Stars are one of the most popular designs for cross stitching, and there are a wide variety of sizes and arrangements included in this section. Detail photos are large enough for you to make your own cross stitched star design, if you like.

Flower designs are a close second to stars in popularity. The **Floral Arrangements** section includes roses, tulips, poinsettias, daisies, and pansies. Also included are stems, leaves, buds, tendrils, ivy, and a trellis.

Assorted patterns comprise the **Potpourri of Designs** section. Living things like butterflies, trees, oak leaves, and kittens can be found here. Also included are inanimate objects like teapots, crosses, candles, bowties, and golf clubs. It's a curious collection of cross stitched designs, with something for everybody.

The final cross stitch category is **Double Cross Stitch**. Commonly referred to as 'chicken scratch', double cross stitches take the basic cross stitched X one step further by adding a cross (+) on top of each X stitch. The result is a thicker and fuller stitch that looks and feels more substantial. Double cross stitches are usually worked on 1/4 inch gingham.

Basic Borders

A basic border of sizable cross stitches highlights this **predominantly pink** apron. Parallel rows travel along the bottom and sides, transforming into a thick band of X's across the deeply pleated top. The square patch pocket, placed to hug the far right edge, is similarly trimmed with cross stitches. The maker of this apron did double duty with both machine hemming and intricate hand hemming along the sashes. Who knows why? $20-30.

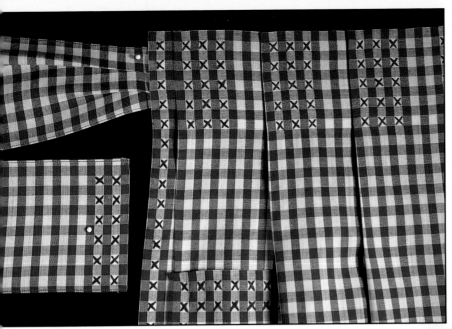

Similar chains of cross stitches parade along the bottom and edges of this bright **blue on blue** gingham design—a thick band at the bottom, narrow rows at the sides. The rectangular pocket is carefully placed to match the background fabric, and each of the six waistline pleats is trimmed with a panel of X's. A dozen stitches have also made their way to the ends of each sash. $20-30.

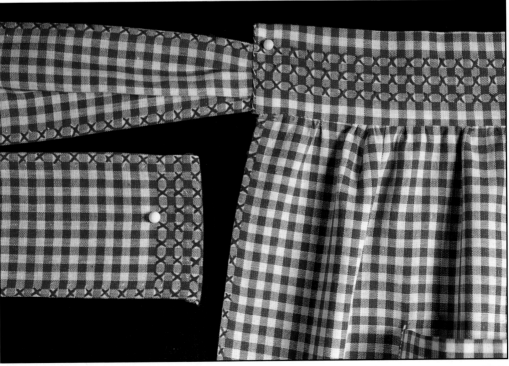

The finer the check, the greater the number of cross stitches. And here is proof. **Two thousand, three hundred and forty-five little red X's**! Along the bottom in a triple wide border separated by single rows, across the waistband and pocket, down both sides of the skirt, and up and down and across the ends of the sashes. All hemming is done by hand in rhythmic white overcast stitches. $30-40.

Ten one inch pleats top this light brown apron of 1/8 inch gingham. Gold and white *crossed* and *uncrossed* stitches comprise the tripartite border, and the rectangular pocket is also outlined in decorative stitches. The waistband has extensions, and there is **a fascinating fabric flaw** near the pocket. $20-30.

Nothing out of the ordinary here. Just **a monochromatic statement** in lavender, in an understated border of spaced cross stitches framed by X's marching single file. Along the banded pocket, too. This basic gathered and pocketed apron was a staple of the 1950s kitchen. $20-30.

Just a minute—what do we have here? **Three colors of embroidery floss**—white, orange, and green—on a background of 1/8 inch navy blue gingham. The skirt and pocket are bordered with a distinctive design of white cross stitches framed with bands of bright orange and green. Thick gathers and a wide band complete the pattern. $20-30.

Twin patch pockets take the spotlight in this beige and white apron. Considerable attention has been given to the decoration and framing of the pockets with dark brown cross stitched designs that drop down from the top. The waistline has **an innovative arrangement of pleats**, but the lower edge has a fairly pedestrian border of *uncrossed* stitches. $30-40.

Tiny *crossed* stitches and huge *un*crossed stitches comprise the rectangular borders on this finely checked (sixteen checks per inch) red and white gingham apron. Triple stranded bright blue embroidery floss was used for all the designs, which are **placed with distinction** along the pocket, waistband, and lower edge. The sashes are entirely faced, and a center seam in the waistband is precisely matched. Look in the *Potpourri of Designs* section for another rare 1/16 inch red gingham apron. $40-50.

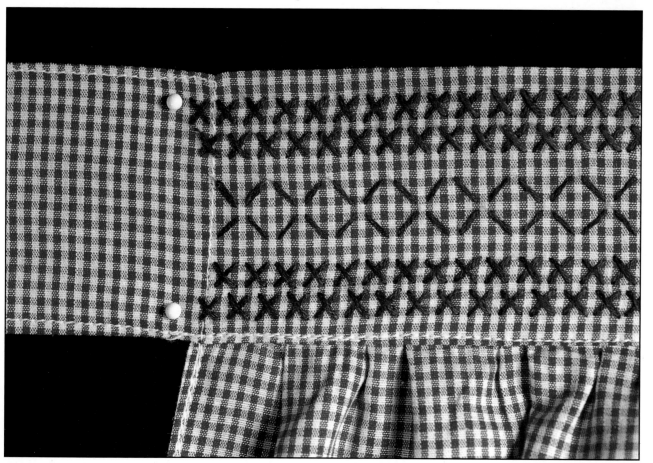

Geometric Borders

This lightly gathered lavender apron features **a dainty panel of cross stitching** along the lower edge and pocket top. Tiny white X's form a rectangular border, which is accented with a row of triangles along the upper edge. Other details include a center seam on the waistband and unusually short sashes. $20-30.

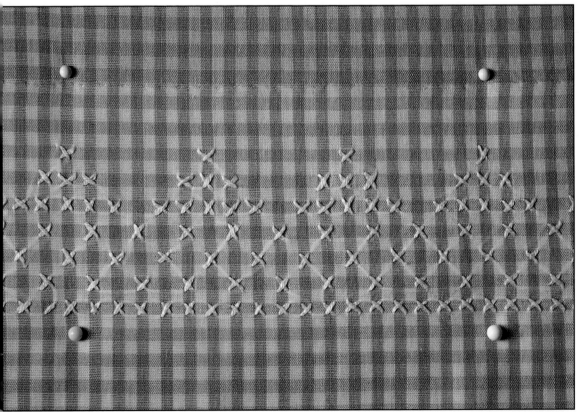

A decorative dual border sets this pine green apron apart from others. A narrow rectangular band and a wider meandering pattern, both in white cross stitches, make a pleasing combination. A tiny band of X's accents the pocket top of this 1/8 inch gingham design. $20-30.

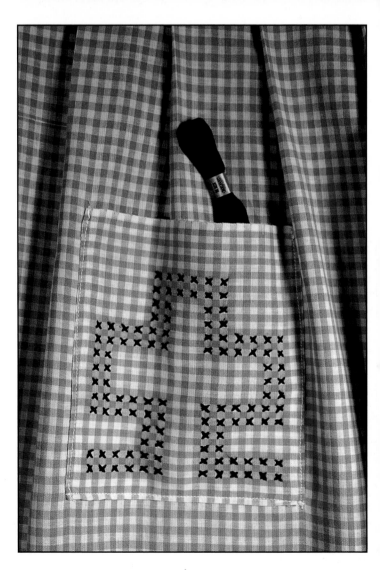

Three rows of black cross stitches march **in and out and up and down** the lower edges of this turquoise apron. Two rows also appear along the upper edge, which is fixed in ten 1/2 inch pleats. An abbreviated crosslike design has been stitched to the pocket, which has an uncharacteristic upper selvedge edge. $20-30.

The addition of **squares, triangles, and diagonals** to parallel rows of black cross stitches make an intricate four inch border on this deep red apron. The upper area is deeply pleated and accented with columns of cross stitches, especially thick at the center. A patch pocket hugs the right edge. Is the cross stitching on the pocket not quite completed? And are those big white *basting* stitches that are still lingering along the waistline? $30-40.

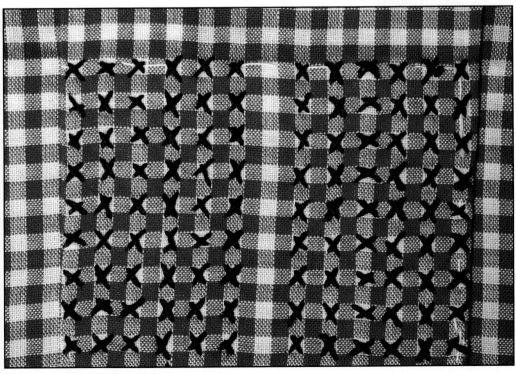

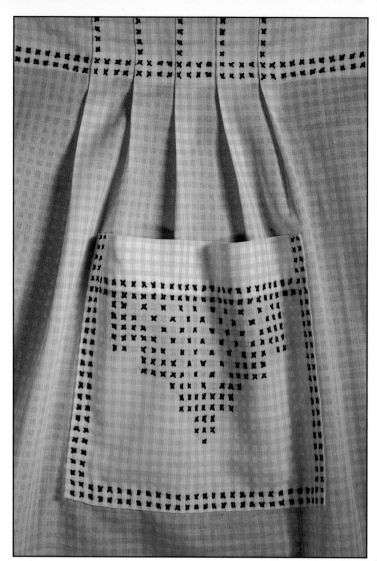

Two **aprons of a similar species** are pictured here in sunny yellow and cherry red. Both have a dramatic lower border of geometric designs suspended from horizontal rows of cross stitches. Each also includes a decorated and outlined pocket design. The yellow apron has ten upper pleats which are anchored and outlined with black X's, as are the ends of the sashes. $20-30.

Twelve upper pleats are totally secured with six rows of cross stitches on this red 1/8 inch gingham apron. The use of **glossy white pearl cotton** lends an unusual luster to the designs. Additional details include single rows of X's along each side of the skirt and an attractive suspended geometric design at the center top. $20-30.

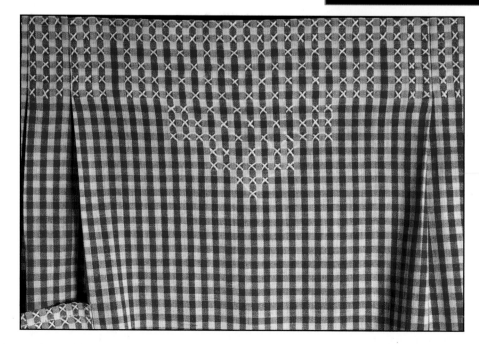

TECKLA PEARSON

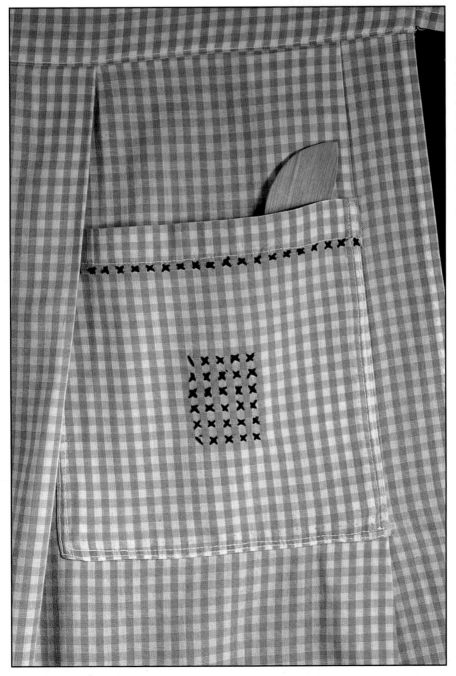

Some will see this as diamonds and triangles; others as squares and hourglasses. Either way, the result is **a rhythmic repetition** captured between single file rows of black stitches. The paired pockets are accented with a single row and rectangle of X's. And yes, this lavender apron could be returned to its rightful owner, whose name is hand stitched to the end of one of the sashes. $20-30.

A chain of **white diamonds** enclosed with black embroidered X's makes an attractive border on the lower edge of this turquoise apron. The square, banded pocket is embellished with cross stitches, as well. Twelve opposing pleats are stitched into the waistband. $20-30.

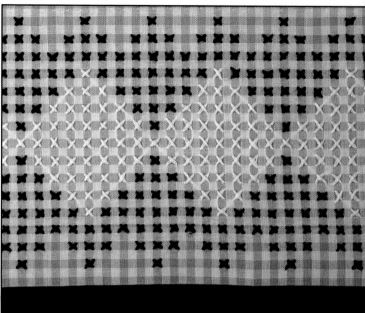

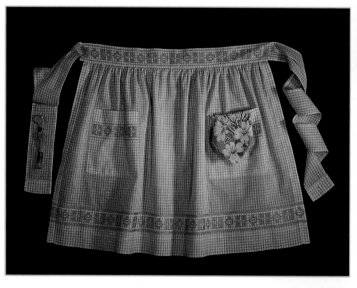

Chains of cross stitched squares and diamonds decorate the skirt, waistband, and pockets of this generously cut apron. Pink is **the color of choice** for both fabric and floss, proving once again, pink's position among the three most popular gingham colors (right up there with red and turquoise). Tiny bands of X's decorate the end of each sash. And the *best* features of this apron—the roomy paired pockets. *Courtesy of Dorothy McMenomy.* $20-30.

Here is one of the very few examples of *printed* (as opposed to woven) gingham aprons in the book. Which means the green checks are **printed on only one side** of the cloth, resulting in a right and wrong side of the fabric. (Woven ginghams essentially have no right or wrong side.) The zigzag border of this apron emphasizes tiny white squares neatly outlined with black cross stitches. The pocket and waistline pleats are outlined and decorated, too. $20-30.

Can you detect the ever-so-subtle suggestion of **positive and negative space** created by the maker of this cherry red apron? The white 'hourglass' shape on the pocket (composed of shiny pearl cotton cross stitches) is transformed into a band of red diamonds when placed side-by-side along the lower edge. This lightly gathered apron also has an extended waistband. *Courtesy of Pat Simonsen.* $20-30.

A Stellar Display

These eight inch stars are possibly the most **expansive stellar renditions** in the apron world. 1/4 inch pea green gingham provides the background for the black cross stitched designs. Individual stars have eight diamond points, each comprised of twelve large X's. A horizontal band of stitches along the lower edge competes this extra long, unpocketed design. $20-30.

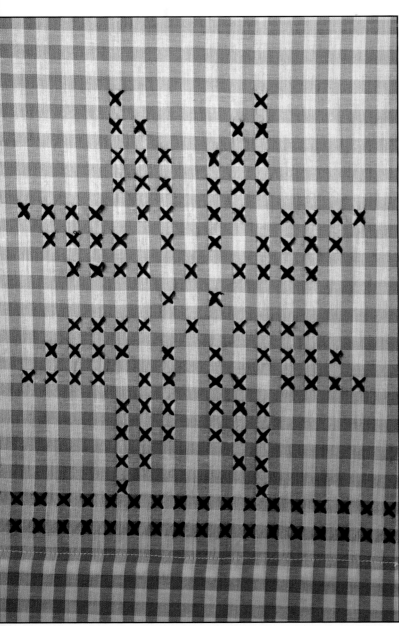

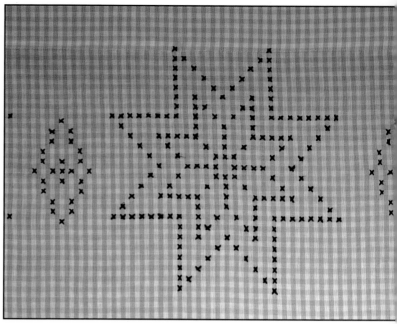

Those pea green stars may be the largest in the lot, but these pink ones run a close second, measuring 6 3/4 inches, point to point. Each star-within-a-star is centered with a radiant motif (Does the one on the right have **parts missing**?) and separated with stylized diamonds. The upper pleats are secured with double rows of black cross stitches, and the sash ends are decorated with a single row. $20-30.

Five similar eight-pointed stars stitched with black embroidery floss decorate the lower edge of this orange sherbet gingham apron. The outlined diamonds create a dramatic **'star-within-a-star'** chained design. A tidbit of cross stitched decoration also appears on the banded pocket of this widely sashed and lightly gathered pattern. $20-30.

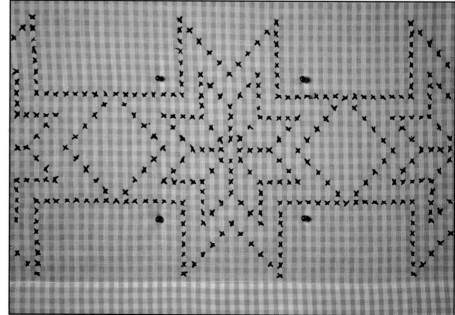

Even more subtle are the **'interrupted' stars** along the border of this lemony yellow and white gingham apron. Each star has been split down the middle and inserted with a substantial 'square-within-a-square' motif. What *really* sets this apron apart from others are the sixty-five miniature pleats, each secured with six white cross stitches. $20-30.

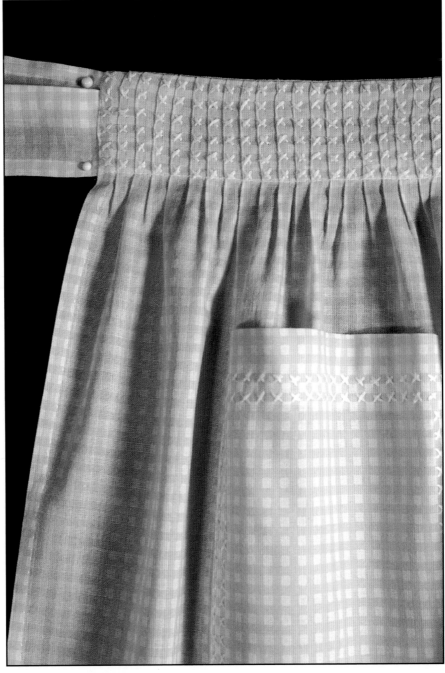

Triangular edging and modified spiral motifs lend to the drama of this sky blue gingham apron. The grand V-shaped pattern culminates in the **suggestion of a gigantic star** at its lowest point. The only additional embellishment is the row of widely spaced cross stitches around the perimeter of the waistband. Perhaps the pocket has been eliminated so as not to interfere with the overall design. $30-40.

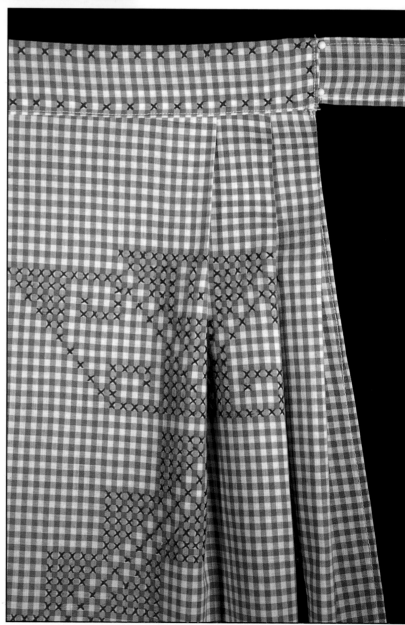

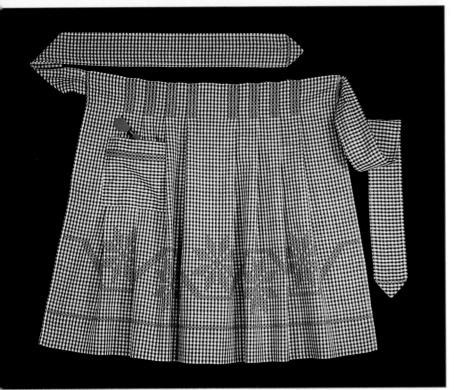

Five **bright red stars** are separated by a ribbon-like interwoven band of cross stitches on this black gingham apron. Single file red X's appear along the lower edge, upper corners, and pointed sash ends. Double rows appear on the pocket, and triple rows anchor the eight pleats. $20-30.

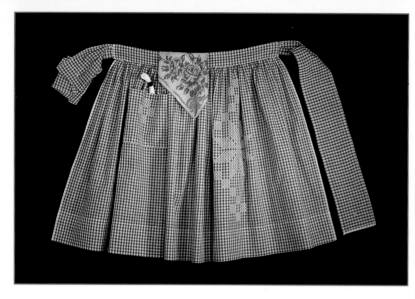

A lone star of eight diamonds is the focal point of this apron. Placed off center and coupled with a chain of tiny squares, the design is complemented with a small grouping of squares on the patch pocket. All cross stitching on this strawberry red gingham apron is done with white pearl cotton. $20-30.

A more elaborate combination of **stars and squares** is found on this 1/8 inch forest green gingham apron. The zigzag style border of stars and a chain of squares hug the lower edge. A full size star framed with a narrow border highlights the square patch pocket. Vertical and horizontal cross stitches secure the shallow pleats along the upper edge. *Courtesy of Vivian Mets.* $30-40.

The makers of the next two aprons were clearly **working from the same pattern**. However, the result is not the same. Both designs are based on an eight-pointed star and a double chain of small squares. The maker of the blue apron opted for larger diamond segments in the stars (twenty-four cross stitches per segment), resulting in an expansive design that drifts off the lower edge and sides. Other details include stitched down waistline pleats (in a single column of X's) and a distinctive pentagonal pocket placed high and far to the right. While the pocket may be a main attraction, the row of machine zigzag stitching along the bottom is the main *distraction*. $20-30.

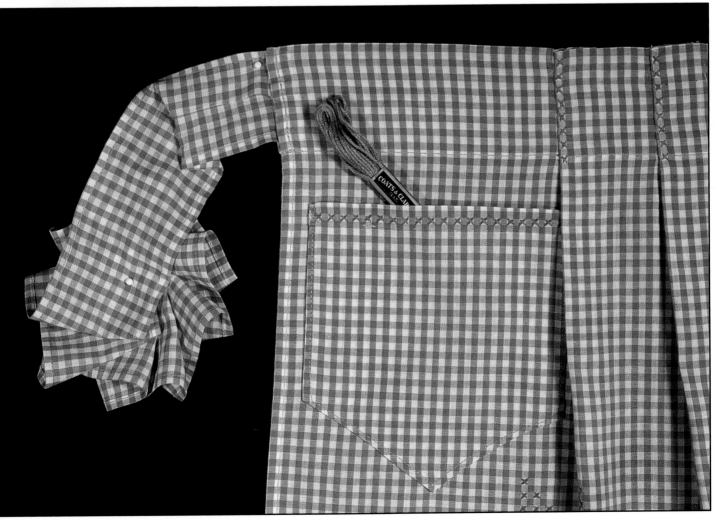

The maker of the lavender apron stitched a smaller star (sixteen cross stitches per segment), and arranged the total design more suitably across the skirt (and the pocket) of the apron. The upper pleats are secured with double rows of X's, and the sides are decorated with stitches that end abruptly at the lower hemline. The real wonder of this apron is that it is **entirely handmade**. All hemming, including up and down the sashes, is done in meticulous overcast or blind stitches. Hand appliqué work is also evident on the pocket. $30-40.

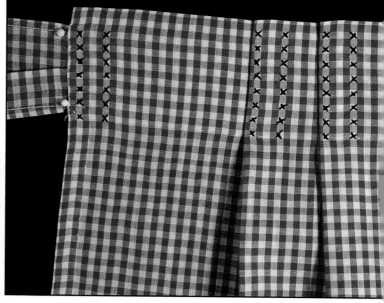

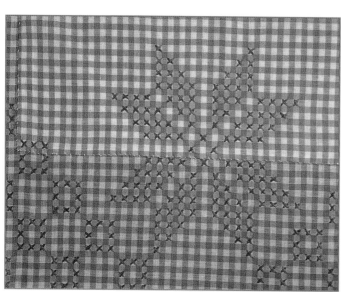

Just when you think you've seen the prettiest star pattern, **a classy five-star design** like this red 1/8 inch gingham shows up. Each black eight-pointed star is separated by an elongated unit, also stitched with black pearl cotton. The pocket and pleated waistline are conservatively decorated with twin rows of black X's, with an added final touch on the sash ends. $20-30.

The five familiar eight-pointed stars take on a few modifications on this **pastel pink apron**. First, each star segment is larger (more black X's). Also, the stars are separated by two parallel lines of cross stitches. The oversize pocket is decorated with a sixth large star. And the final decorative touch is modestly stitched on the waistband. $20-30.

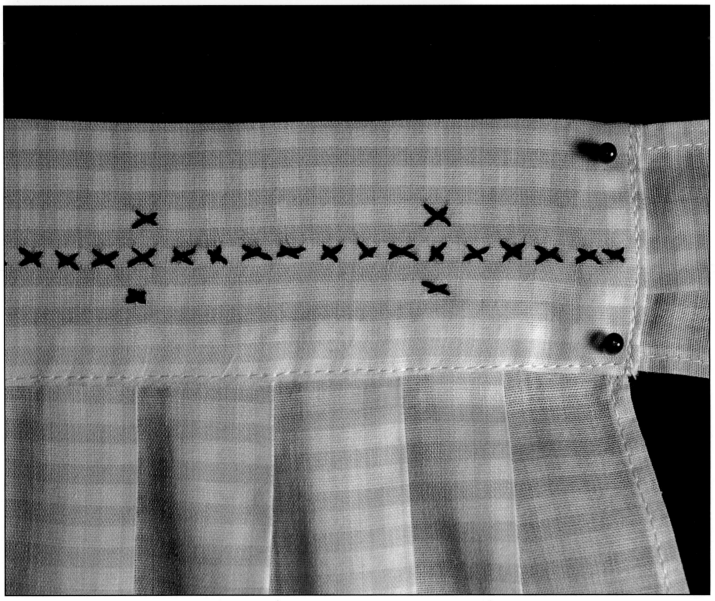

Floral Arrangements

No two alike is the claim I've been making all along about gingham aprons. Well, it's mostly accurate. **No two *exactly* alike** is closer to the truth. Here are two aprons with the same construction pattern—1/8 inch pink checks, a pleated waistline, a massive cross stitched design of flowers and leaves, and no pocket. Their makers were obviously working from the same set of instructions. On closer inspection, several differences can be found. The lighter shade of pink apron has eight mirrored pleats at the top. Its upper stitched border has smaller central motifs (only five stitches each). The lower panel of stemmed and staggered flowers is a study in itself. Although the flowers are uniform in size and shape, occasional variations occur in the placement and composition of the leaves. Some are lacking a second row of cross stitches, some are ill-placed, and others seem to have gone missing! $20-30.

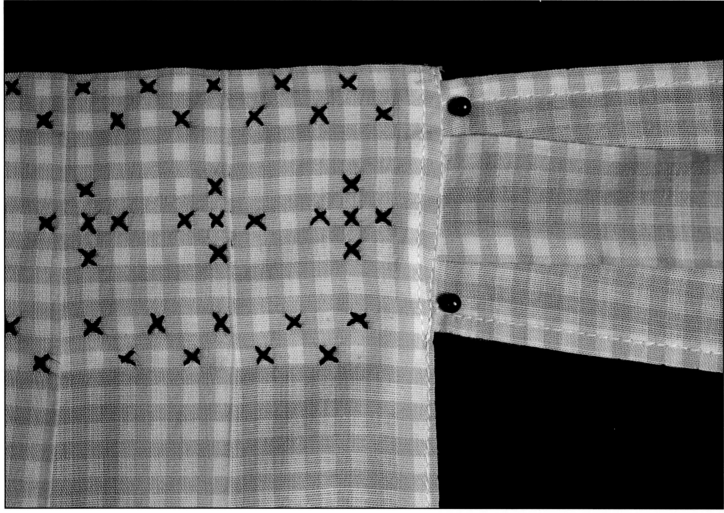

The **deeper shade of pink** apron has six mirrored pleats at the top. Its upper border has larger central motifs (twelve stitches each), plus an extra row of stitches at either end. An added decorative feature is the band of cross stitches on the end of each sash. The wide floral panel has been stitched with far more precision, although variations (intentional or unintentional) can be found. The rhythm of two and three leaves along each stem is uniform, the few inconsistencies being an isolated misplaced stitch or missing row. I'm reluctant to label these *missing* or *misplaced* stitches as errors. *Design variations* is the designation I prefer. In addition to revealing the workmanship and individuality of each maker, the variations may also reflect the differences found in the natural world of flowers and leaves. $20-30.

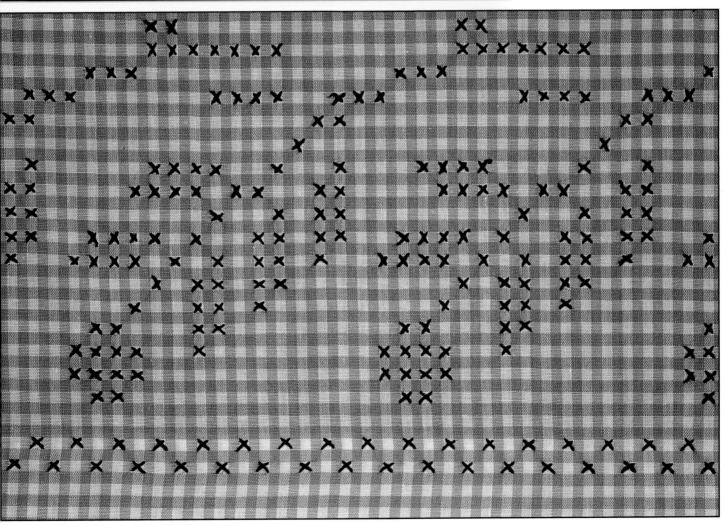

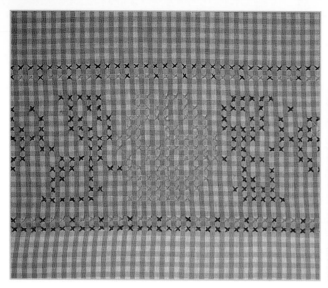

Three **passionate pink roses**, each flanked by tiny rosebuds and deep green leaves, grace the bottom of this gathered apron. The tripartite border design is framed with parallel rows of cross stitches. Fragments of this cross stitched border also appear on the pocket and at the end of the pointed sashes. A well-placed piecing seam on the waistband is nearly undetectable. $20-30.

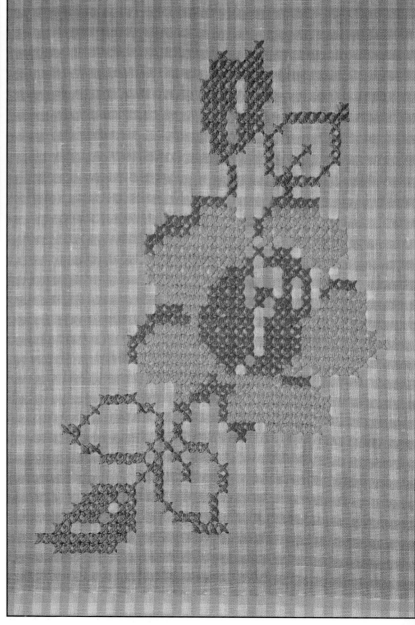

Five magnificent roses adorn the skirt of this 1/8 inch gingham design. Densely cross stitched with triple stranded embroidery floss, the blooms and leaves appear particularly robust and lifelike. A panel of deep pink crossed and light pink uncrossed stitches highlight the waistband, and a plain six inch square pocket floats atop the lightly gathered skirt. $30-40.

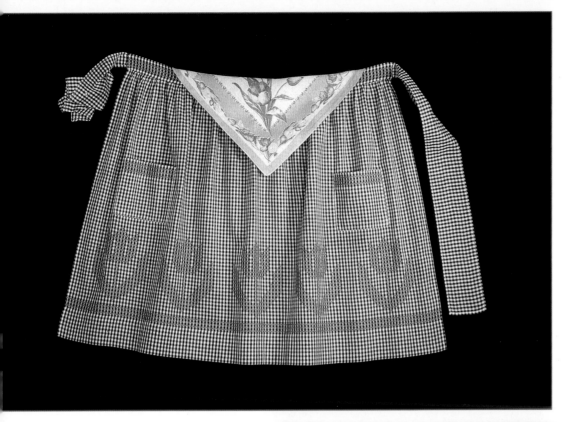

You're likely to **think spring** when wearing this tulip-bordered gingham apron. The use of black fabric and dark shades of red and green floss for the cross stitches (each obliterating a white square) lends an especially somber tone. A three-rowed border tops the hem of the skirt, the bands of the twin pockets, and the waistband. The stitched designs are quite subtle graphically and play tricks with the eye. $30-40.

And then you can **think holidays** in this poinsettia laden pattern. The bright and luscious flowers and leaves are accomplished by using triple stranded red and green embroidery floss. Each flower is accented with a pale yellow center. Other details included sparingly decorated twin pockets, a gathered waist, and exceptionally short sashes. $30-40.

Although brown may not be the first choice of color for a gingham apron, it's clear that this monochromatic effort is an especially successful one. The trio of large roses is neatly bordered, the pocket perimeter is carefully cross stitched, and the upper pleats are also adorned. Add to that the embellished sash ends, and the result is **first class design**. And lest you think this is the only brown apron in the book, keep looking. There are at least five others. $30-40.

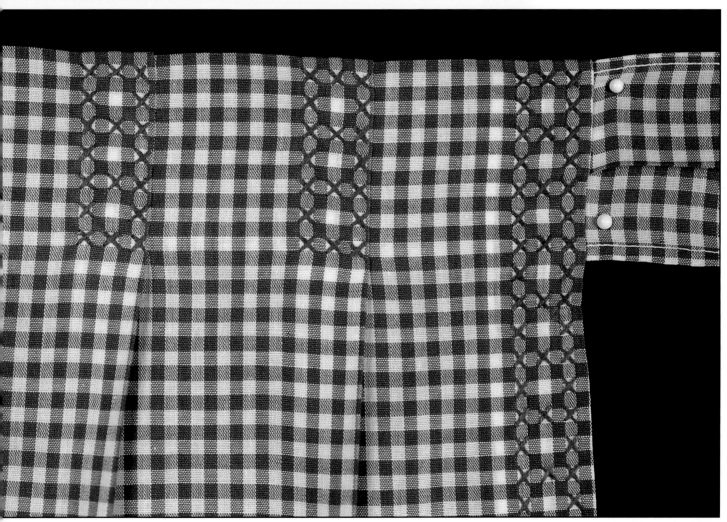

Another gingham color that is comparatively rare is purple. This plum-colored fabric makes a regal background for the three **yellow star flowers**, which are accented with small red centers and large green leaves. A band of cross stitches outlines the skirt, which also has an unadorned pocket that is nearly invisible. $30-40.

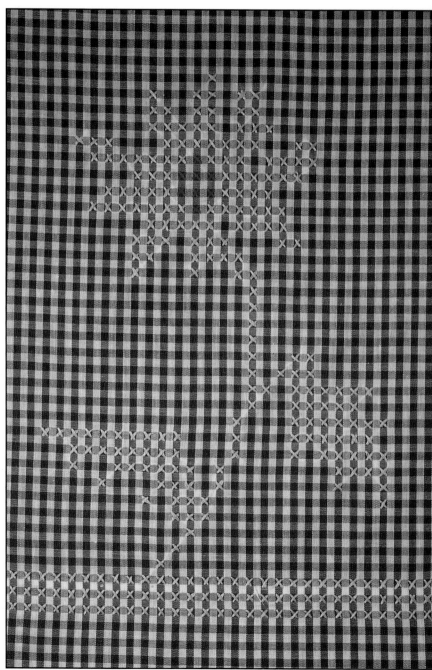

Set diagonally and off center, this sweeping design of green five-leaf ivy winds its way through a trellis of white cross stitches. The choice of light colored embroidery threads and pale pink gingham makes this composition especially low contrast. An oddly shaped pieced pocket reveals that this is **not just another pink apron**. The center seam and V-shaped top entry set this pocket apart from all others in the book. $30-40.

And finally, a stroll through **a patch of pansies** stitched in lavender, yellow, pink, blue, and shades of purple. A sandy brown 1/8 inch gingham serves as the background for this subtly cross stitched arrangement. A decorated pocket and gathered waistline complete this delicate design. *Courtesy of Betty Wilson.* $30-40.

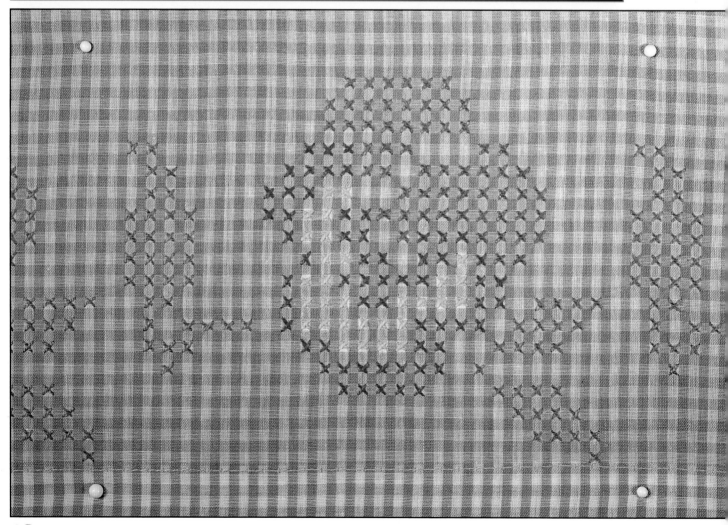

A Potpourri of Designs

Seven teapots wend their way across the lower edge of this generously cut lavender gingham apron. Complete with **handles, lids, and spouts,** each pot is rendered in triple strand black embroidery floss. The square patch pocket is decorated with an extra teapot. Eighteen shallow pleats are anchored and topped with a row of black cross stitches. Bring on the crumpets! $30-40.

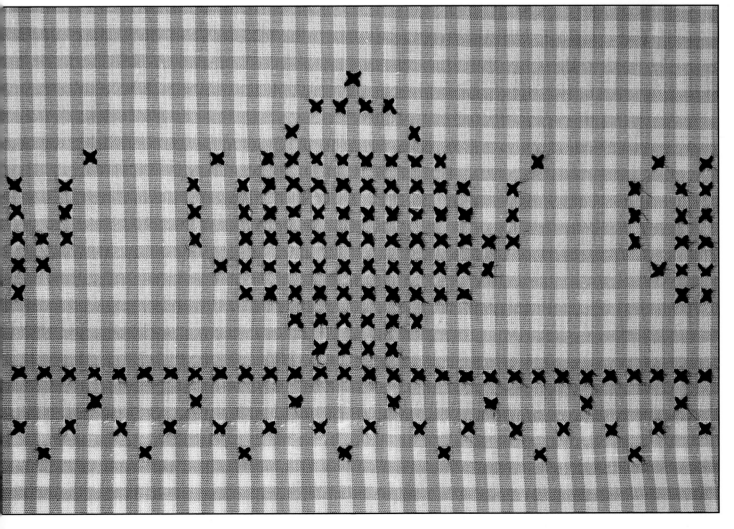

The dark combination of navy blue gingham and black embroidery floss results in the shadow-like designs on this apron. **Four playful kittens** and a potted plant make up the primary design. The U-shaped pocket and wide sashes are accented with single rows of black X's. Ten pleats with triple row stitching top the apron. Can you find the lingering basting stitches on the pocket? $30-40.

You're likely to get **that holiday feeling** when wearing this pleated turquoise gingham design. Six evergreen trees are stitched with medium green floss and decorated with multicolored ornaments. Each tree is topped with a barely discernible white star. A decorative panel highlights the lower edge, pocket, and waistband. $30-40.

Traditional festive greetings prevail on this deep green checked apron. Three elegant white glowing candles rest in bright red holders. The letters N-O-E-L are stitched in red embroidery floss and nestled between the candles. This pocket-free loosely gathered design is surely among the prettiest in the book. *Courtesy of Betty Wilson.* $30-40.

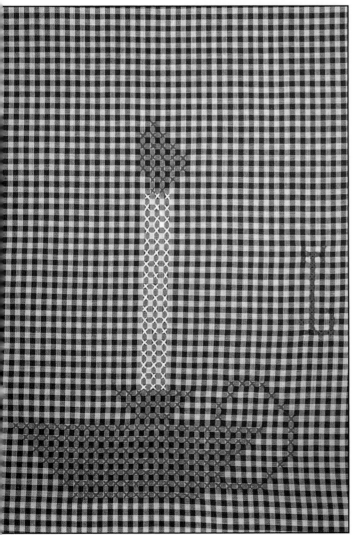

Life-size green oak leaves and two-tone brown acorns comprise the overwhelming arrangement on this golden gingham apron. Six pleats are clustered on either side of the waistline, each anchored with brown cross stitching. Similar X's trail along the sides of the apron, around the pocket, and along the entire length and breadth of the sashes. $30-40.

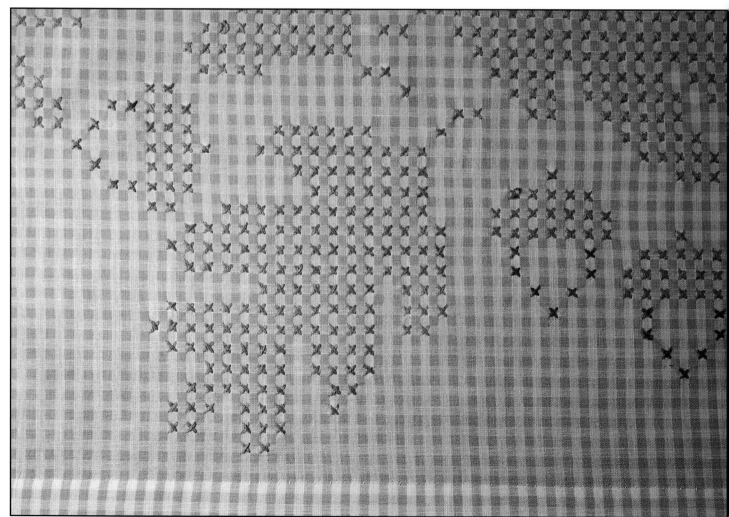

Wedgewood blue gingham and white pearl cotton lend a stated elegance to this gathered and banded apron. Five **larger-than-life** bowties (or are they butterflies?) grace the deeply hemmed (five inches) lower edge. Cross stitches appear in two sizes—small ones for the bowties and sash ends, large ones along the waistband, both sizes on the pocket. $30-40.

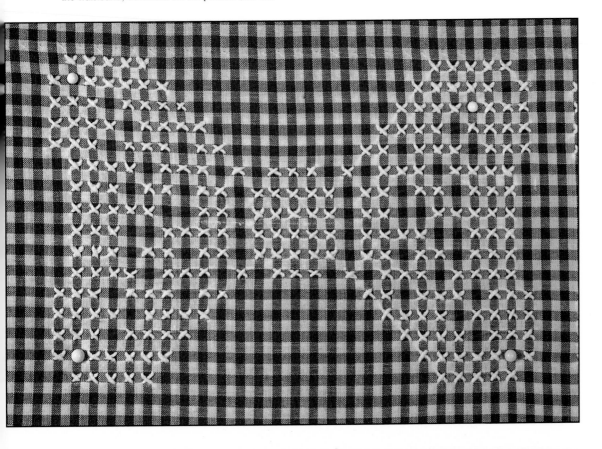

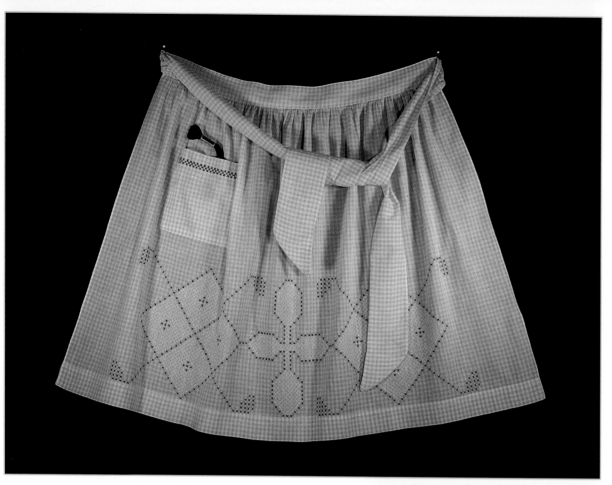

An unusual tripartite border of **unidentified objects** dominates this delicate pink gingham apron. Fine pearl cotton in white and black is used in the nine inch wide design. A sole accent of cross stitches tops the pocket. So, what shapes do *you* detect—diamonds, hexagons, golf clubs? $30-40.

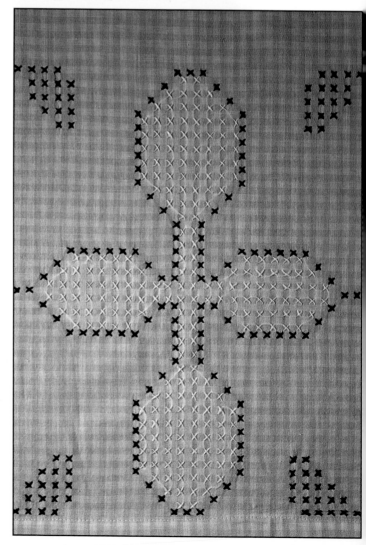

The choice of white embroidery floss results in an unobtrusive but attractive border of chained **squares and crosses** on this turquoise apron. Twelve shallow pleats along the top are anchored with dual columns of white cross stitches. The square pocket remains unadorned. $20-30.

Are there really 4,309 cross stitches on this apron? If so, it takes the honors for **'the greatest number of stitches.'** Of course, the primary reason is the tiny 1/16 inch checked fabric—scads of territory to insert the tiny white double-strand embroidered stitches. And if that isn't enough, the maker of this apron did every portion by hand, from the wee hemming stitches up and down the sashes to the finely appliquéd pocket. What further intrigues me is the illusion of curves created by the tiny X's. $40-50.

There is no mistaking these big brown butterflies with their **seven inch wing spans**. Each insect and flower is thickly stitched with brown embroidery floss. The paired pockets and waistband are accented with bands of large cross stitches. My mother found this widely hemmed and thinly gathered cotton/polyester apron in a drawer in her church kitchen. I'm sure it has witnessed many church suppers, funerals, celebrations, and launderings. *Courtesy of the women of the First Baptist Church of Waupaca, Wisconsin.* $30-40.

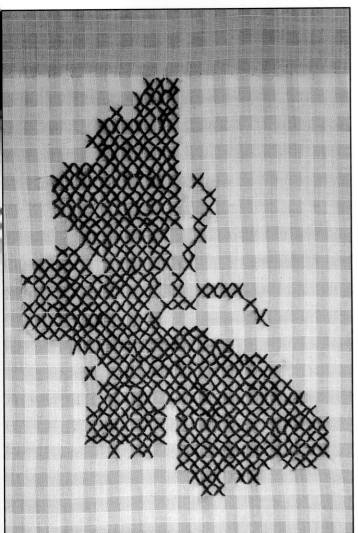

A touch of old-time religion makes its way into the kitchen with this sunny yellow **'Give Us This Day'** apron. Each word is carefully stitched in green and highlighted with brown embroidery floss. Large seven inch crosses stand guard at each end. Notice the thick waistline gathers and extra long and wide sashes. $30-40.

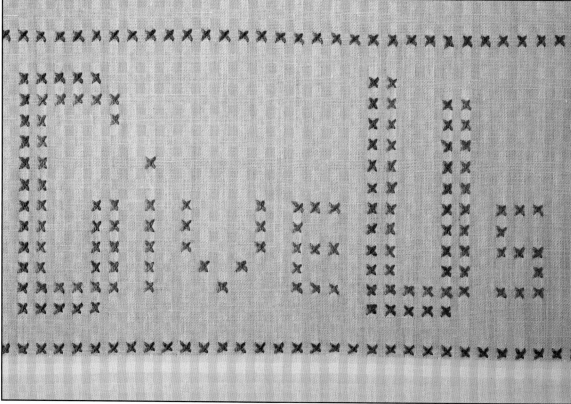

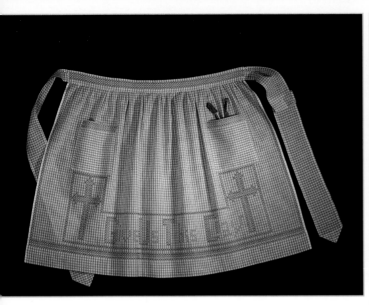

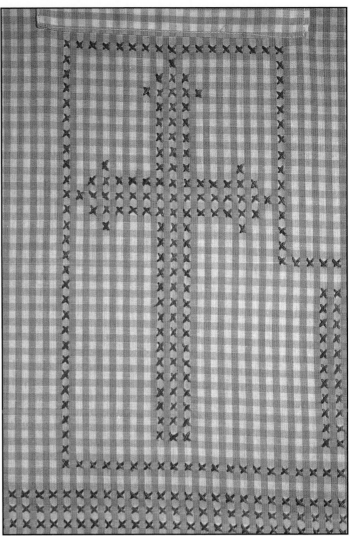

The maker of this **prayerful pink** apron chose bright blue and pink embroidery floss for accent colors. In addition to the four word inscription, carefully placed rows of cross stitches have been added along the waistband, pocket, and skirt. Instead of the customary 1/4 inch side hems, the unturned white selvedge serves as the finished edge. $30-40.

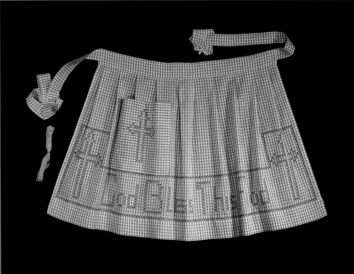

The ever popular turquoise apron returns here in reverential form. The blessing—**'God Bless This Food'**—is stitched in black and highlighted with bright tangerine. In addition to the two large crosses, a third slightly smaller cross highlights the huge (more than seven inches square) patch pocket. Eight pleats and extremely long narrow sashes complete the apron. $30-40.

Double Cross Stitch

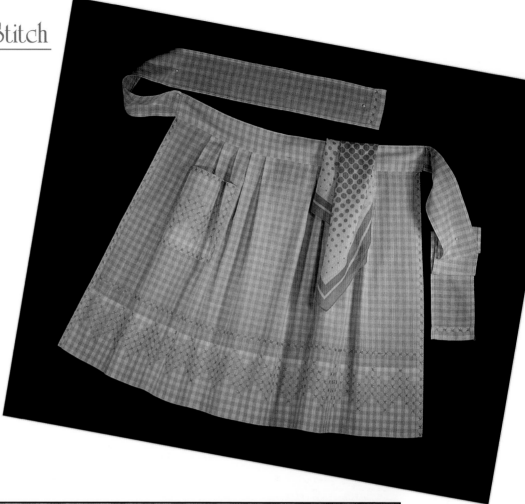

Bright pink pearl cotton stitches and pale pink 1/4 inch gingham are the main components of this 'chicken scratch' apron. The border design zigzags across the lower edge of the apron, topped and sided by rows of single stitches. A similar motif is stitched on the six inch pocket. This standard pleated and banded apron also has five double cross stitches on the ends of the sashes. $30-40.

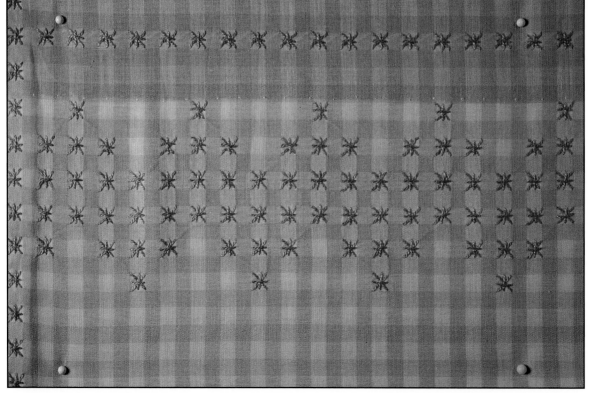

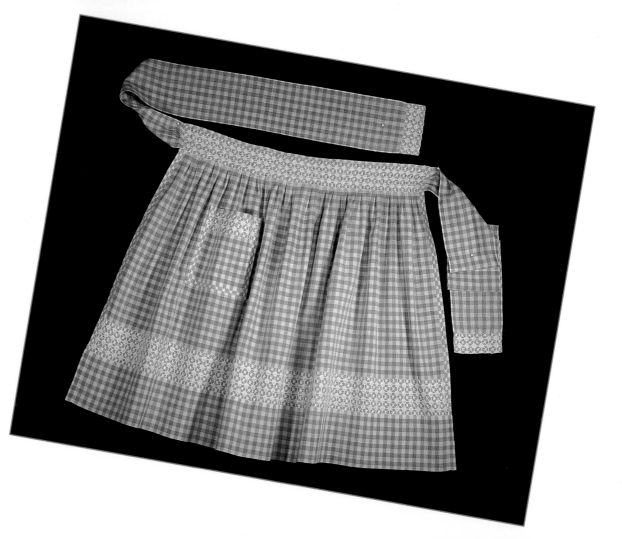

In addition to using a heavier pearl cotton, the maker of this turquoise apron added a grid of **chain-like stitches** between the double cross stitches. Each double cross stitch is placed on a dark gingham square; each circle chain stitch (a diamond, really) is placed around a white gingham square. The result is a saturated design area of whiteness composed of both angular and circular elements. The thirty-two waistline pleats are secured with the same design, as are the ends of the sashes (front and back!) and the patch pocket. $30-40.

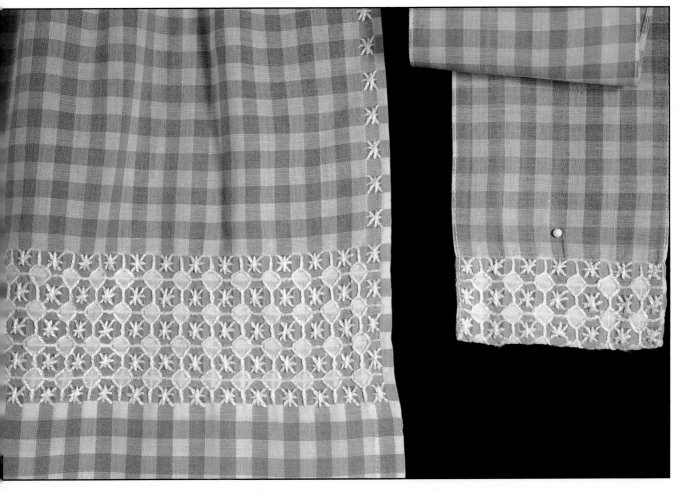

Brown and white pearl cotton make **a bold statement** on this crisp orange gingham apron.
The contrast of dark and light threads in the tripartite border is especially eye-catching.
Narrow design panels stitched in brown top the pocket and waistband. $30-40.

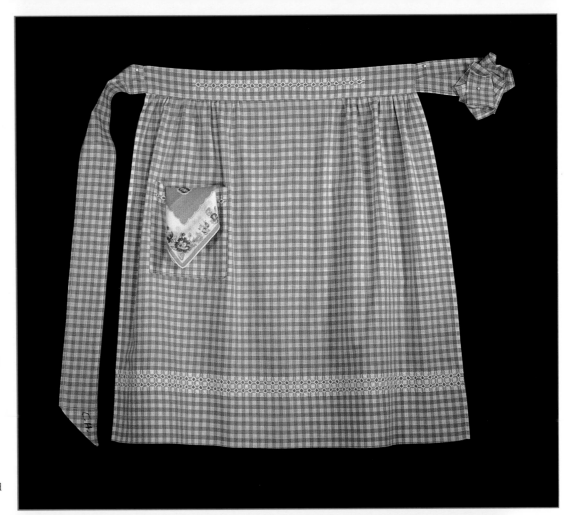

Yet another turquoise apron—this one **simply and sparingly accented** with white-on-white double cross stitches and diamond chains outlining the *dark* gingham squares. (Compare this with the preceding turquoise /white apron which has diamond chains outlining the *white* squares.) An abbreviated design panel is centered on the waistband and pocket. And the owner/maker has inscribed initials (C. H.) on the end of a sash. $30-40.

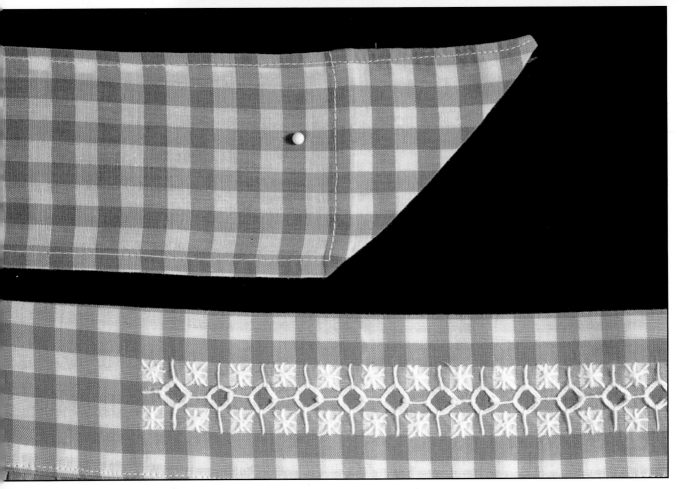

Black gingham aprons are not as rare as one might expect. At least ten are included in this book—this one back to the basics of **just black and white**. A three inch wide panel of stitchery traverses the lower edge, and narrow strips dominate the gathered waist and patch pocket. $30-40.

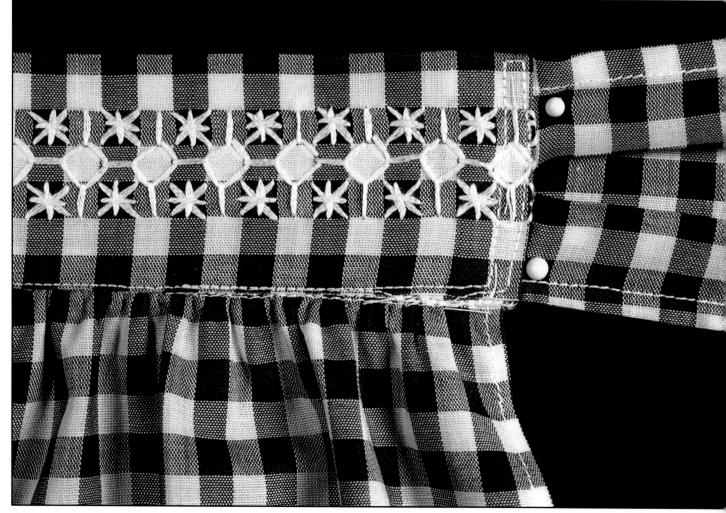

All eyes are on the border of this gathered turquoise number. The cleverly designed expansive border of white and aqua diamonds is stitched with triple strand embroidery floss. And that's all there is—no extra stitchery designs, and not even a pocket. But wait! Can you detect the subtle change of color in embroidery thread? $30-40.

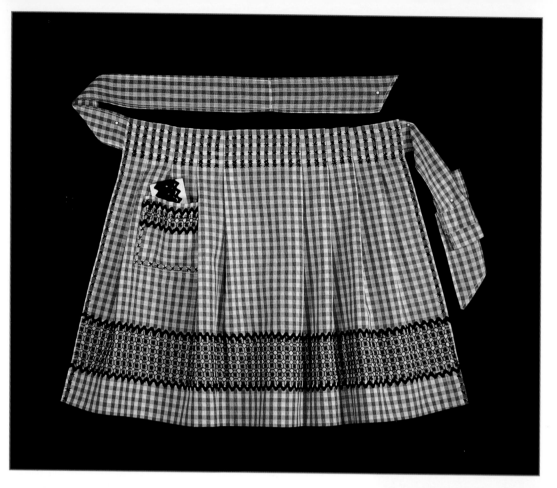

Black rickrack grabs one's attention on this strawberry red gingham design. In addition, there is **a proliferation of black 'chicken scratches'** (some rather erratically placed) and diamond stitches. Possibly among the showiest of aprons in this section of the book, this pleated design also has pieced sashes. $30-40.

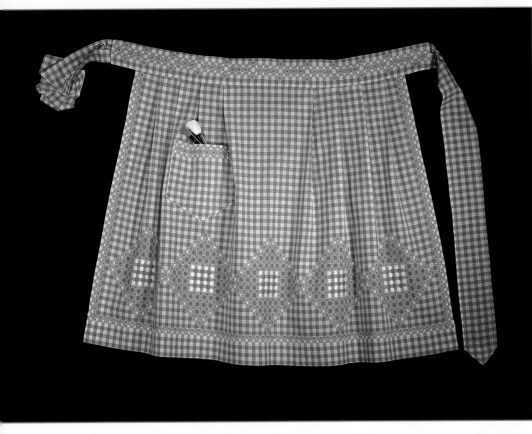

So what's different about this turquoise apron? First, the pentagonal pocket. Second, the white and aqua satin-like stitches that create the distinguished woven checkerboard pattern in the center of each of the five large diamonds. Add to that a myriad of double cross stitches, and the result is **a lavish one-of-a-kind design**. $40-50.

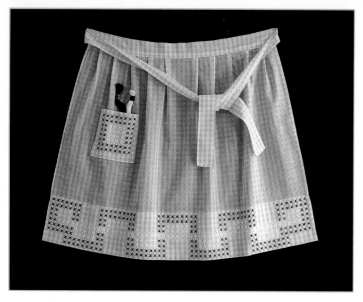

Sunny yellow gingham is decorated with a meandering pattern of black and white embroidery floss on this pleated apron. The fully lined pocket is similarly ornamented with large black and white double cross stitches and white chain stitches. Sure to warm up any kitchen or dining room. *Courtesy Janet Carson.* $30-40.

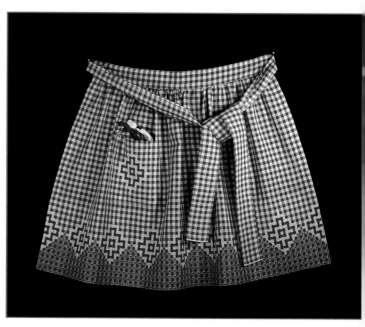

Squares set on point lend an especially dramatic note to this cherry red apron. The *darkened* lower area is accomplished by stitching red double cross stitches over the plain white squares. Alternate red and white stitches create a prominent album-like pattern in each diamond. Generous sashes (each a full yard long) and a suitably decorated pocket complete this gathered apron. $40-50.

Section Two:
Rickrack

This section of the gallery includes gingham aprons with rickrack as the primary embellishment. These are further subdivided into three categories according to the size of rickrack and combination with other decorative techniques.

The eight aprons in the **Regular Rickrack** section have 1/2 inch mid-size rickrack as the main adornment. It is usually attached in parallel horizontal rows. A variety of colors, including gold and silver metallic are shown. Different styles of stitching, including both hand and machine, are utilized to secure the rickrack.

Miniature and Jumbo Rickrack are the main ingredients of the second group of aprons. Miniature (narrow) rickrack makes a welcome contrast with both regular and jumbo rickrack. Bold and bossy, jumbo rickrack is frequently applied to 1 inch wide gingham or used in a tucking technique.

Added elegance is the obvious result in the group of gingham aprons with **Rickrack and Cross Stitch Combinations**. While rickrack alone may be sufficient, the addition of cross stitches yields particularly fine designs. Some cross stitching is just plain X's. Others are 'uncrossed' stitches. Still others are cleverly anchored with cross-bar stitches. One especially delightful design includes feather stitching.

Rickrack-adorned gingham aprons are not confined to this section of the book. Many are scattered throughout **Section Three: Design Techniques**. Be on the lookout for all sorts of combinations of rickrack with pulled thread, smocking, Teneriffe, zigzag borders, and organdy.

Regular Rickrack

This brightly decorated turquoise apron stands out from among the others for a couple reasons. First, it includes an unprecedented **four different colors of rickrack**, each row flawlessly hand applied with long stitches along the center and tiny stitches on each rickrack point. Second, it is the only 1/4 inch gingham design in this sub-section. The remaining examples are 1/8 inch gingham. Other design elements include paired sections of pleats at the waist and rickrack accents on the pocket. $30-40.

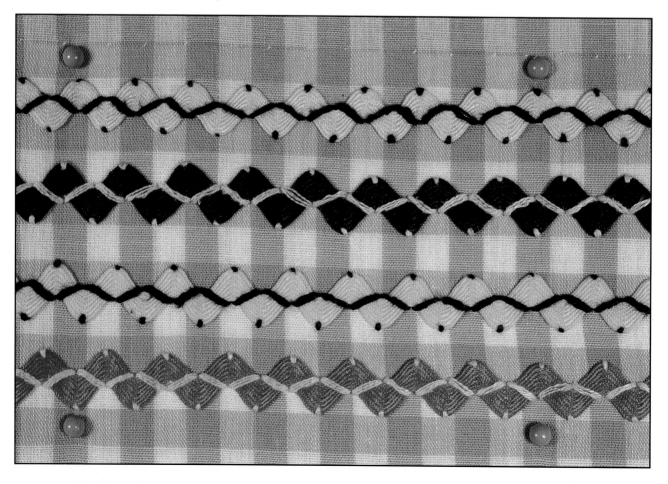

This classic black and white checked and gathered apron is **an exercise in minimalism**. Black rickrack trails down the sides and along the bottom of the skirt. The solitary accent is on the banded pocket. All rickrack is attached with machine stitching. $20-30.

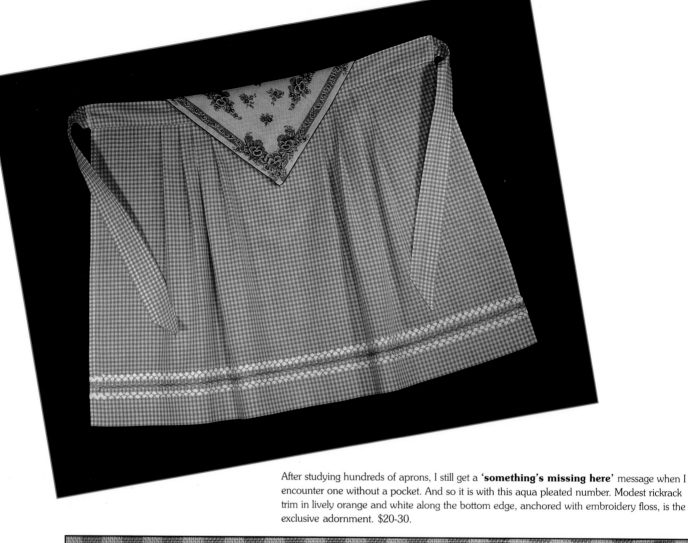

After studying hundreds of aprons, I still get a **'something's missing here'** message when I encounter one without a pocket. And so it is with this aqua pleated number. Modest rickrack trim in lively orange and white along the bottom edge, anchored with embroidery floss, is the exclusive adornment. $20-30.

Miniature pink rickrack adds design interest to this finely checked brown apron. Combined with regular rickrack in two shades of green, the result is a pleasing five part border, sections of which are repeated on the pocket and waistband. Each row of rickrack is hand stitched in contrasting thread. The **abbreviated waistband design** also sets this apron apart from others. $30-40.

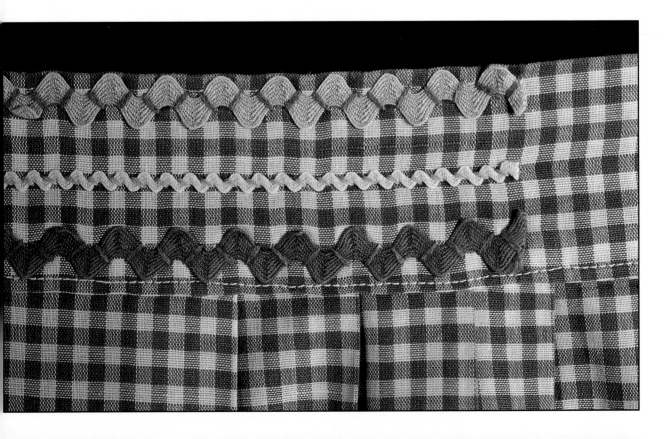

Dual-colored rickrack adds a special touch to this aqua apron. Actually it's tricolored (white and yellow with flecks of black). Combined with traditional white and yellow rickrack, each row is hand stitched with contrasting colors of floss (pink, green, and blue). The rectangular pocket is uncharacteristically shallow—four inches deep, five inches wide. $20-30.

Miniature white rickrack and tiny purple cross stitches have been combined with standard rickrack on this pleated lilac apron. **Deep purple** was the color of choice for the hand application of the rickrack—done in elegant elongated stitches. A bit of cross stitching also accents the hems of the sashes. $30-40.

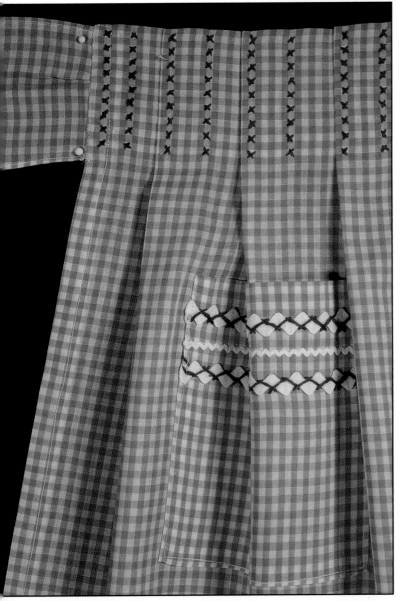

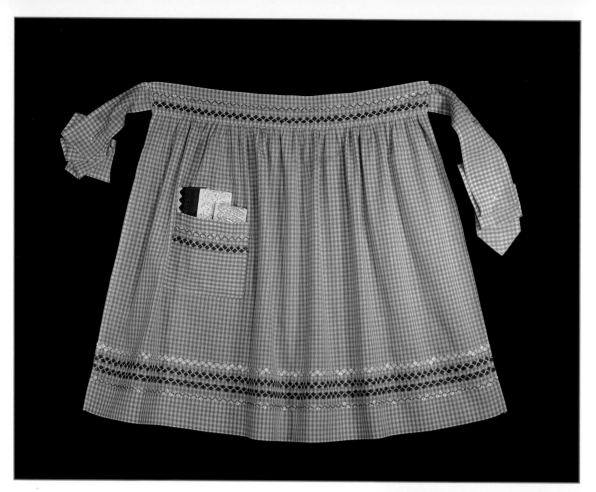

We can **add a little glitz** with metallic rickrack—silver, in this case. Actually we have three styles of rickrack here, two metallic and one regular. Each is secured with cotton pearl in brown, white, or pink. The pocket and waistband of this gathered turquoise apron are also neatly decorated. $30-40.

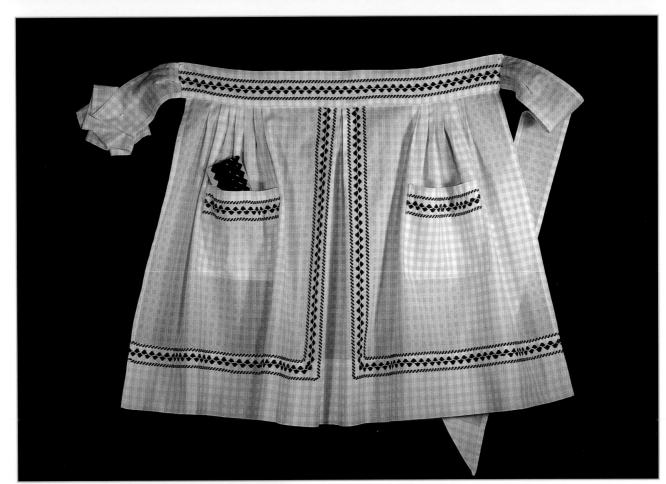

Dark chocolate brown and buttery yellow pair up in this dramatic rickrack design. 1/4 inch yellow checks provide the backdrop. Regular size brown rickrack is flanked by rows of miniature rickrack, all secured with triple stranded yellow embroidery floss. The paired pockets and the opposing designs separated by the center box pleat make a strong visual statement. Watch in the upcoming section for more examples of miniature rickrack. *Courtesy of Betty Wilson.* $30-40.

Miniature and Jumbo Rickrack

Red appears to be the predominant color in this section. Especially *wide* red gingham checks to accommodate the *wide* rickrack. First off is this **showy lipstick red apron**. Notable details include: regular width red rickrack anchored with white embroidery floss, jumbo white rickrack anchored with red floss (points tacked, as well), and sixteen dramatic mirrored one inch pleats resulting in a white central panel accent. What's also unusual is the 'left sided' pocket. What's more unusual is that this apron is *entirely* hand stitched (including the appliquéd pocket and the minute hem stitches along the sashes)—truly an admirable artistic and technical accomplishment. $40-50.

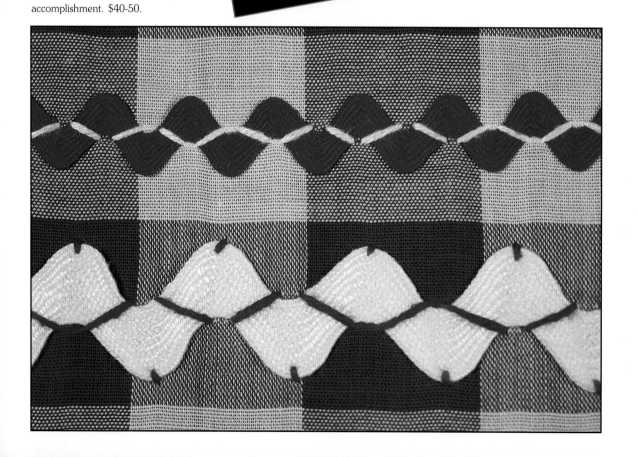

This black and white 1/4 inch gingham apron comes to life with the introduction of **red, white, and blue—**red jumbo rickrack, white embroidery floss (triple stranded), and blue regular rickrack. White is also the choice for the modified 'chicken scratches'—each composed of three, rather than four stitches (lacking a horizontal cross stitch). This apron is a gift from a friend, Lois Osterberg, and was made by her mother. $30-40.

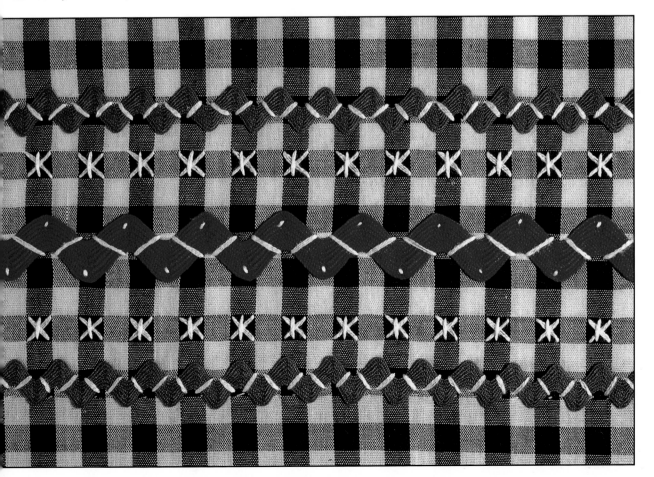

Enter next a diversion from the usual gingham designs. This one is a *printed* 1/4 inch check. **Printed gingham** can be distinguished from woven gingham by comparing both sides of the fabric. In woven gingham, the front and reverse sides are *essentially the same*. In printed gingham, the check is printed on the top side only, the back side remaining much lighter, clearly the *wrong* side of the fabric. This modest pleated apron is highlighted with a tripartite border of regular white rickrack and miniature blue rickrack, all of which is machine stitched. No handwork on this number, not a stitch. $20-30.

And now, surprise, a diversion from the predominance of red! Brown and yellow take center stage in this one-way pleated one inch gingham apron. Bright yellow jumbo rickrack is flanked with miniature rickrack, each secured with brown embroidery floss. A distinctive vertical stitch anchors the points of the oversize rickrack. The border design floats high above the wide hem and generous pocket, and the narrow waistband is **jam packed with rickrack**. $30-40.

We go now from one of the narrowest waistbands (the one inch brown) to one of the widest (three inches red). In addition, the waistband extends beyond the sides of the apron skirt, into uncommonly wide sashes. What makes this apron especially memorable is the jarring contrast of **wide checks and narrow rickrack**. The three deep pockets formed cleverly along the lower edge, and the accented vertical panels in the center and along the sides make this apron a keeper. $30-40.

Miniature and jumbo white rickrack join forces in parallel rows along the pocket, upper edge, and lower edge of this wide checked turquoise apron. All rickrack is anchored with turquoise embroidery floss, using elongated slant stitches and tiny tacking stitches. **A single row of smocking** adds a lovely accent to the upper portion of the apron, smocking being a technique rarely found on one inch ginghams. (An entire section of this book is devoted to smocked aprons. Look there for eight more examples and styles of smocking.) *Courtesy of Betty Wilson.* $30-40.

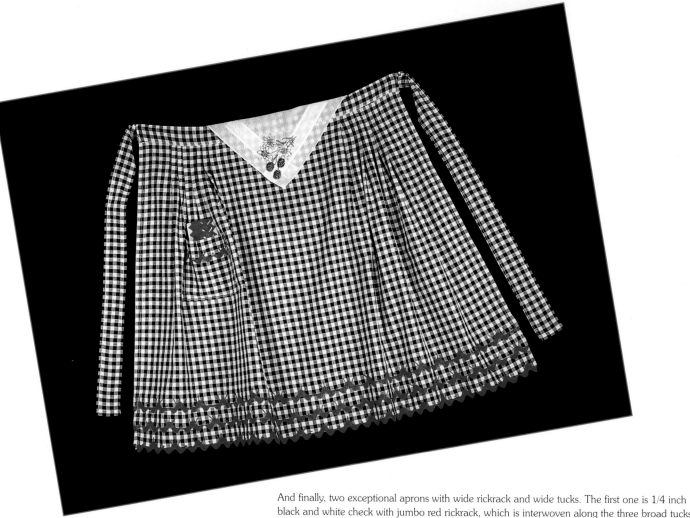

And finally, two exceptional aprons with wide rickrack and wide tucks. The first one is 1/4 inch black and white check with jumbo red rickrack, which is interwoven along the three broad tucks on the lower edge and on the pocket. French knots and a trio of elongated stitches in red pearl cotton are used to keep the rickrack in **a perpetual state of suspension**. Other details include a diminutive pocket and barely visible groupings of pleats on each side. $30-40.

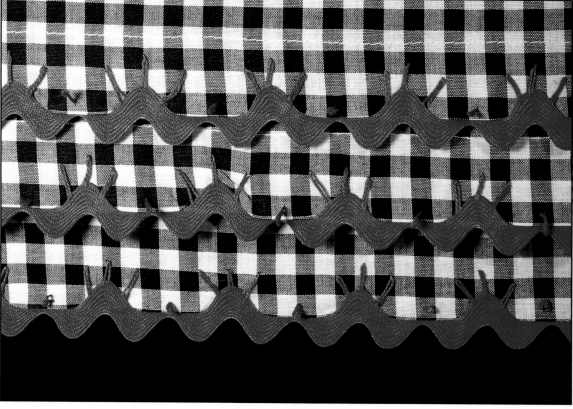

And now, the finale—**big rickrack, big tucks, and big checks**. Again, a triple row of tucks along the lower edge, each inserted with jumbo white rickrack and secured with French knots and a single vertical stitch. This gathered apron has a more suitably sized banded and trimmed pocket. $30-40.

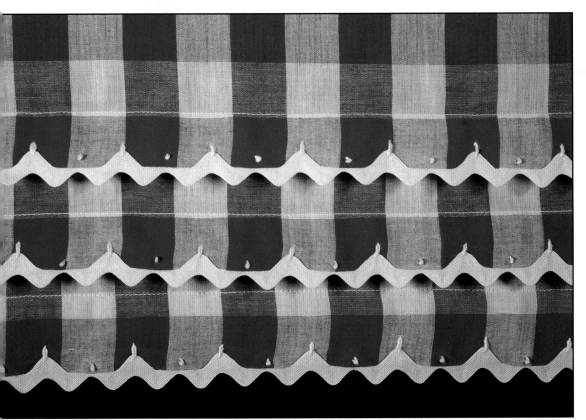

Rickrack and Cross Stitch Combinations

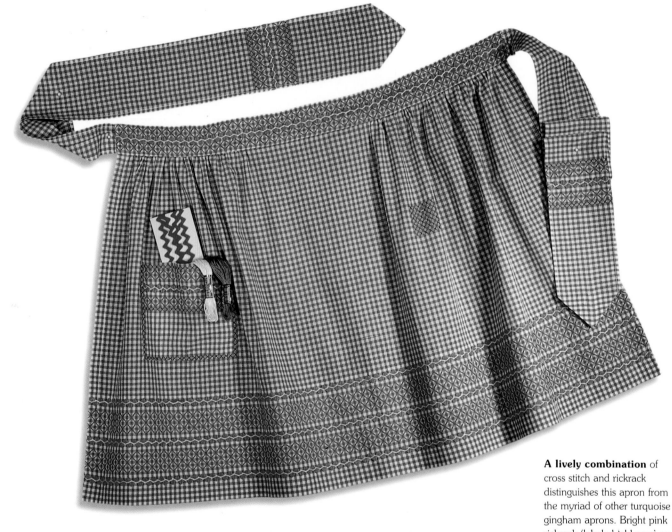

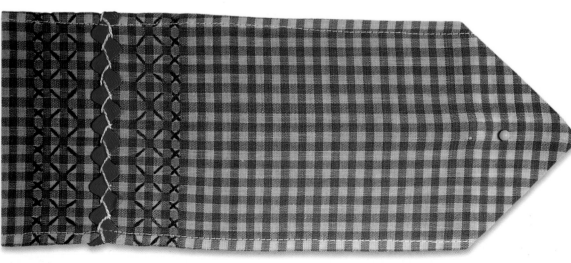

A lively combination of cross stitch and rickrack distinguishes this apron from the myriad of other turquoise gingham aprons. Bright pink rickrack (labeled 'old rose' on old rickrack packages) is secured with white pearl cotton. The hand-worked stitches in the border and waistband are uncrossed. Regular cross stitches appear on the pockets. So what's really different about this apron? One, the sizable decorations on each sash, placed six inches from the pointed ends. Two, the miniature cross stitched design (1 1/2 inches square) on the skirt of the apron, perhaps positioned to camouflage a flaw in the fabric. Look closely. $30-40.

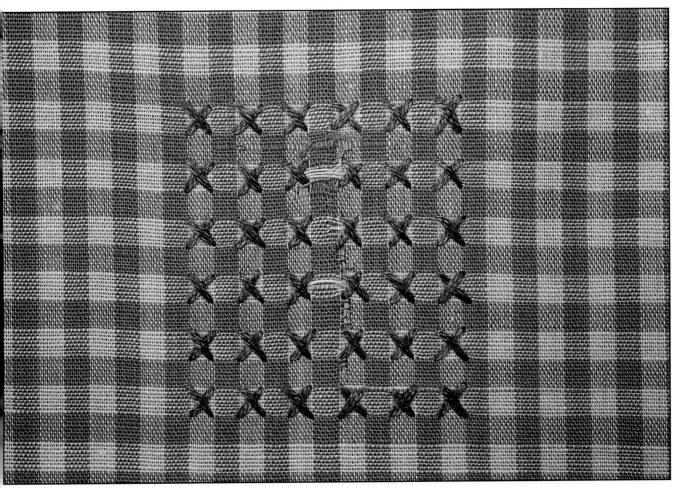

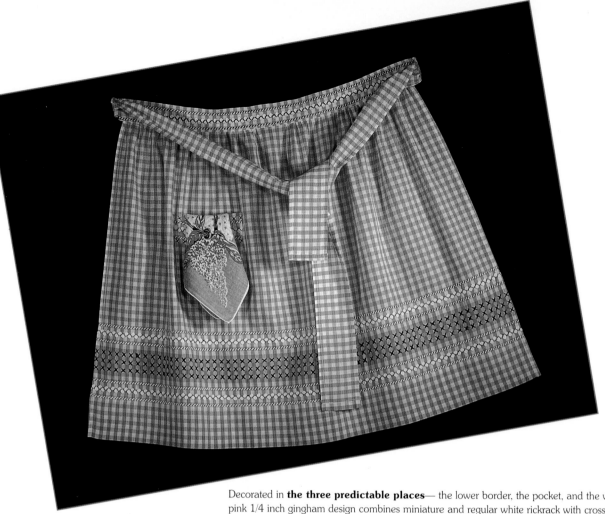

Decorated in **the three predictable places**— the lower border, the pocket, and the waistband— this pink 1/4 inch gingham design combines miniature and regular white rickrack with cross stitching. The three rows of chunky X's in black heavy duty two-ply pearl cotton lend a weighty feeling to the lower border. All rickrack is carefully anchored with lighter weight pearl cotton. The skirt of this lightly gathered apron is longer than most—twenty-two inches (five inches longer than the previous apron). $30-40.

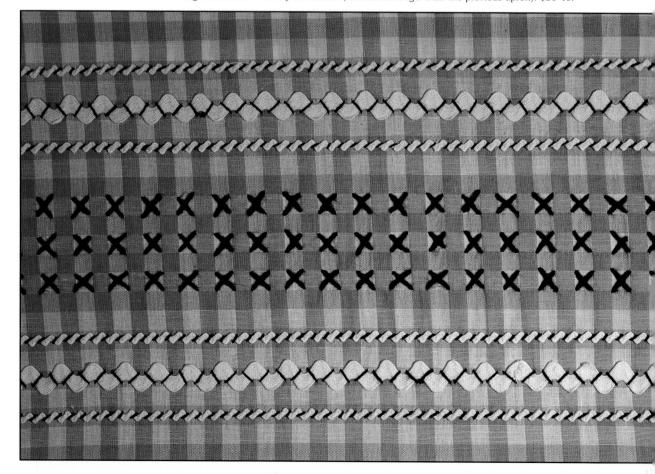

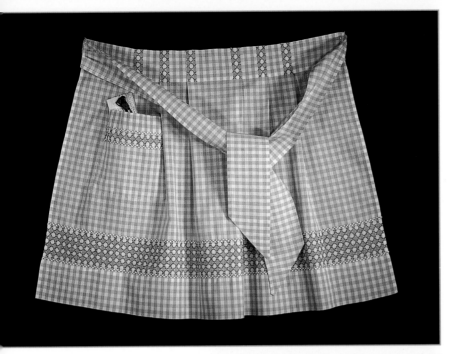

Six one inch pleats top this **caramel colored gingham** design, each secured with fourteen cross stitches. The three inch lower border is crowded with similar stitches, each worked in triple strand brown embroidery floss and 'anchored' with a tiny white stitch at the center. One of my references calls this stitch a 'cross-bar filling'. It is accomplished by first working diagonal stitches (i.e., the cross stitch X), then adding short horizontal stitches at each crossing of the diagonal threads. Rows of hand applied miniature white rickrack outline the lower border and the pocket. $30-40.

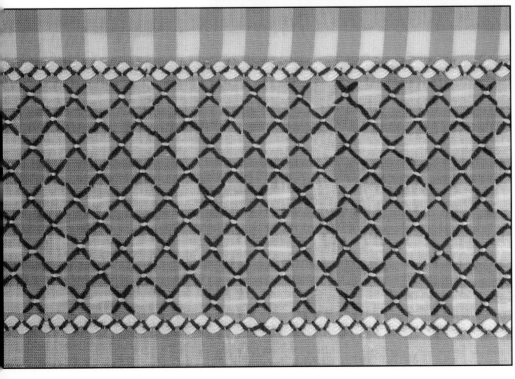

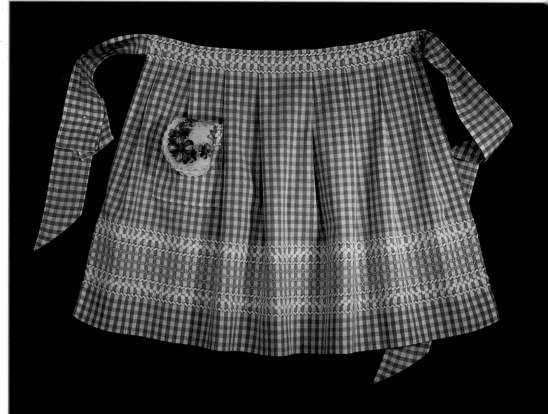

White rickrack (in two sizes) mingles with white cross stitches on this handsome sky blue gingham apron. Each white X is secured with a tiny blue center stitch, and all rickrack is hand attached with the same triple strand blue embroidery floss. All told, it's a pleasing and unaffected **study in blue and white**. $30-40.

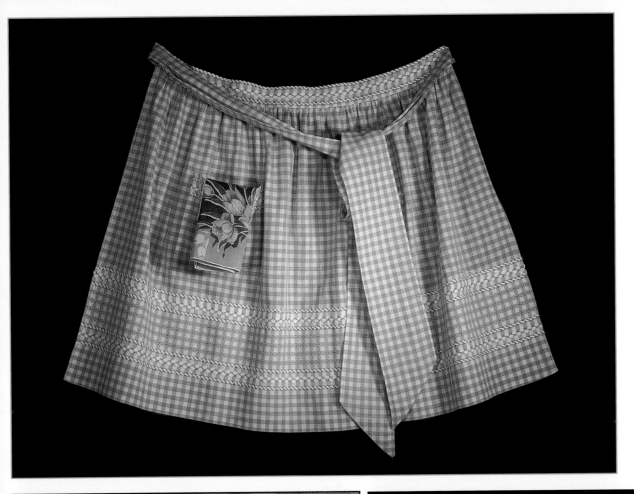

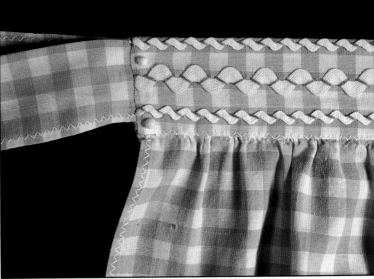

The maker of this apron was clearly **operating from the same set of instructions** as the maker of the previous blue apron. Waistband and pocket detailing are identical. The lower border is nearly identical. The main variances on this butterscotch gingham apron are the gathered waist and extensive use of machine zigzag stitching on the side hems, waistband, and sashes. $30-40.

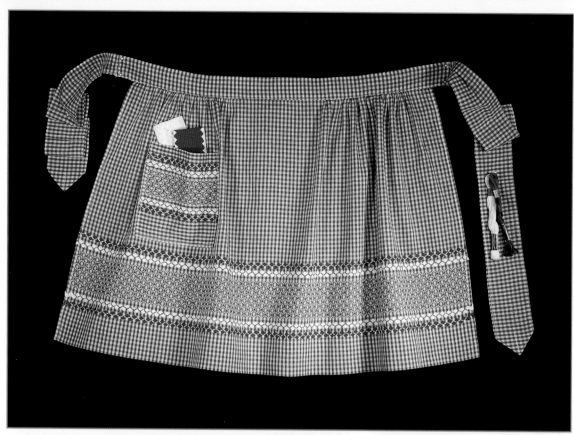

You need look no further for **a masterpiece combination of rickrack and cross stitch**. Generous rows of rickrack—in brown and white—and *large* fancy X's stitched in white, each accented in the center with *tiny* brown X's, create a showy five inch border. Rich cinnamon brown and pure milky white never looked so good. $40-50.

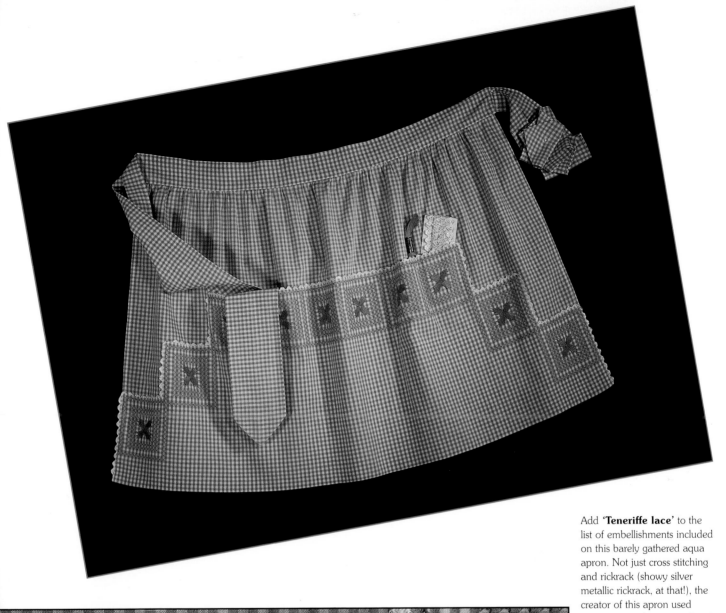

Add **'Teneriffe lace'** to the list of embellishments included on this barely gathered aqua apron. Not just cross stitching and rickrack (showy silver metallic rickrack, at that!), the creator of this apron used turquoise pearl cotton to hand weave ten Teneriffe designs. Each measures 1 1/2 inches square and is surrounded by dual rows of wee cross stitches. The 'stairstep' layout not only lends a sense of drama, but also conceals two generous pockets, each measuring 6 1/2 by 5 inches. (An extensive gallery of aprons with Teneriffe designs can be found in Section Three of this book.) $40-50.

Feather stitching and a vintage handkerchief with birds—what an attractive way to end this section of rickrack and cross stitch combination aprons! This 1/8 inch brown checked apron has white rickrack, uncrossed stitches in two colors, plus two rows of hand worked **decorative feather stitching**! The wide band of uncrossed (slant) stitches is worked in alternating rows using white and aqua embroidery floss. Rickrack attention is also given to the pointed sash ends. $40-50.

Section Three:
Design Techniques

This final portion of the gallery is overflowing with gingham aprons with outstanding design techniques. Although cross stitch and rickrack are the predominant means of embellishment on checkered aprons, several other needlework procedures have been used in the past.

Pulled Thread designs (also known as Drawn Work) have showy see-through panels where rows of horizontal threads have been removed. Remaining vertical threads are then grouped, overlapped, and secured with embroidery floss or pearl cotton. Often worked in combination with delicate cross stitching, the result is airiness and elegance.

You're in for a surprise if you thought **Smocking** was the domain of little girls' dresses. Gingham aprons and smocking also go hand-in-hand. This group of eight smocked designs includes some of the most handsome in the book. Bias cut fabrics, fastidious tucking, rickrack trim, and ruching lend added pizzazz to the smocked patterns.

The world of **Teneriffe Lace** design was opened wide when it was coupled with gingham apron patterns. Adapted from a style of lace making (also known as wheel lace) from the island of Teneriffe (Canary Islands), these mysterious little woven designs are perfect embellishments for 1/4 and 1/8 inch gingham checks. What I consider one of the most breath-taking apron designs in the book can be found in this Teneriffe section.

Nothing quite compares with the graphic visual impact of the aprons in the **Stairstep Borders** section. The zigging and zagging of the gingham fabric along the sides and bottom of these aprons is most impressive. Special effects such as golden rickrack, commercial decals, and cross stitching have been added to many of the patterns.

And finally, the place to look for all those aprons that are **In a Class By Themselves**. These include printed ginghams, convertible aprons (into a bonnet, no less), marriages of gingham and organdy, appliqué designs, and crocheted edgings. Practical styles such as gathering aprons, drawstring aprons, and waitress style aprons are also pictured. And as I continue collecting aprons, I'm certain to find others to add to this section of assorted styles.

Pulled Thread

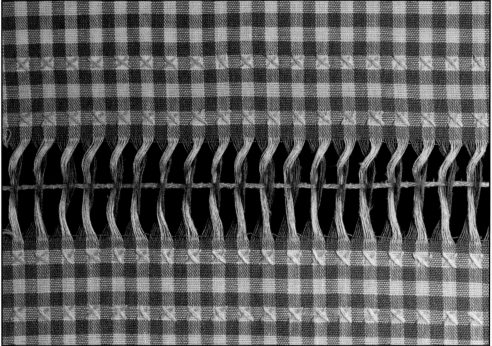

Once again, **understated elegance** in shades of blue. Eight rows of horizontal threads have been 'pulled'. The remaining one inch band of vertical threads has been interwoven with six-stranded light blue embroidery floss. Paired rows of tiny blue cross stitches flank the drawn work. What really sets this apron apart from others is the petite round bottom pocket, which is also trimmed with X's. $30-40.

Drawn thread work never looked more elegant. Each band of drawn work is only 3/8 inch wide. The remaining threads are crisscrossed and interwoven with white pearl cotton. Multiply this by three and separate the bands with rows of dainty white cross stitches (also pearl cotton) for a lovely delicate border of **sunny yellow and snowy white**. $30-40.

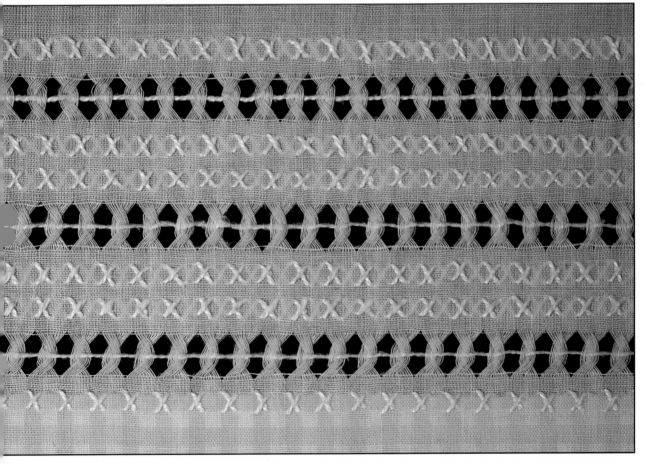

Drawn thread work and cross stitching come together with **rare grace and beauty** in this cherry red gingham apron. Among the most expansive of pulled thread designs, this border measures ten inches wide. The waistband is also saturated with *uncrossed* stitches. The maker has attended to every detail, including hand worked stitches along the sashes and pulled thread designs on the sash ends. Don't tell anybody there's no pocket. $40-50.

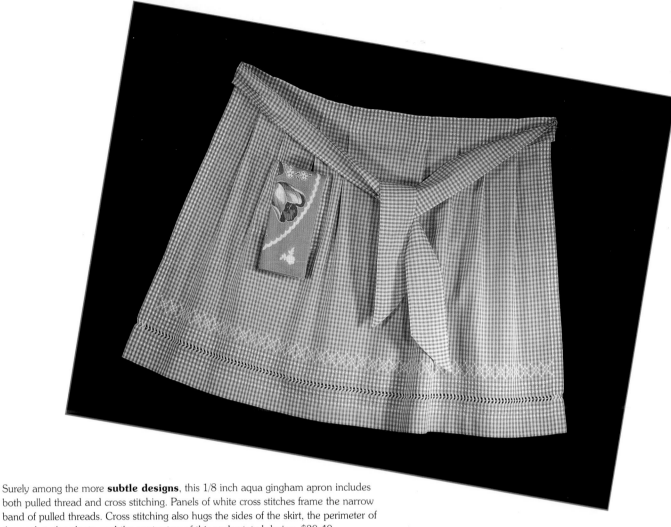

Surely among the more **subtle designs**, this 1/8 inch aqua gingham apron includes both pulled thread and cross stitching. Panels of white cross stitches frame the narrow band of pulled threads. Cross stitching also hugs the sides of the skirt, the perimeter of the pocket, the pleats, and the center top of this understated design. $30-40.

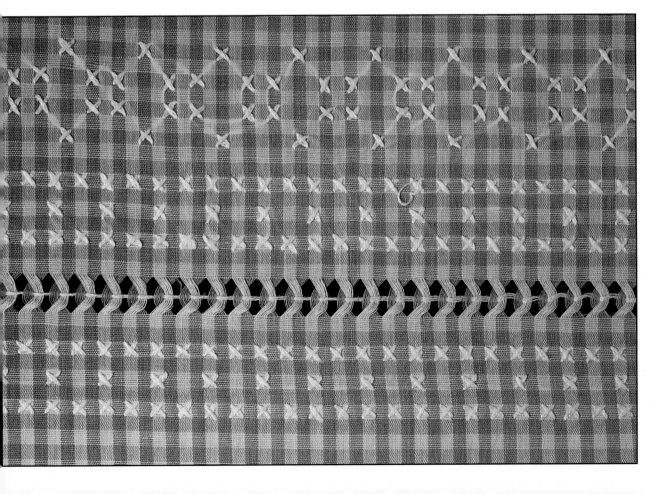

Next we move on up to bright red 1/4 inch gingham, where cross stitches have a **larger than life** appearance. The bands of pulled thread are 3/4 of an inch wide, the remaining vertical threads grouped and interwoven with six-stranded red embroidery floss. The large cross stitches are also executed with full stranded floss. Pocket and side embellishments complete this lipstick red design. $30-40.

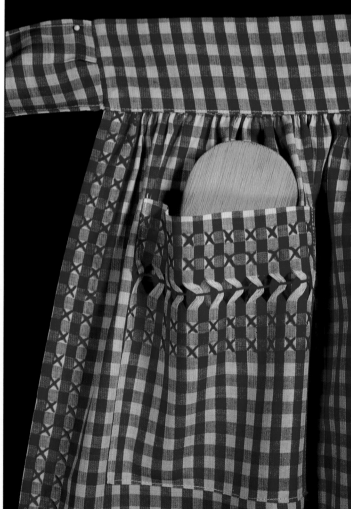

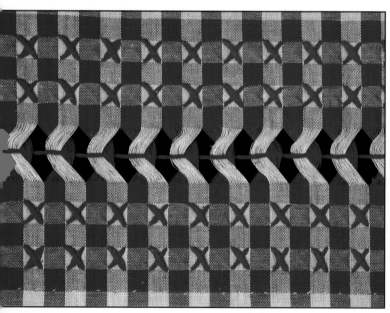

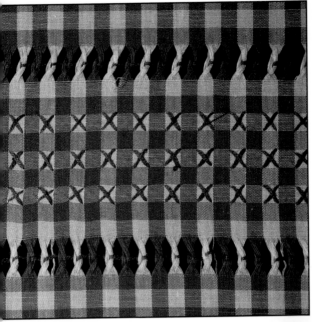

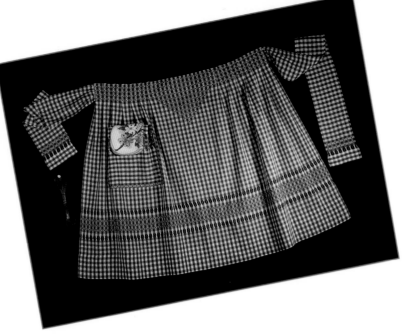

Pulled thread work appears in three places on this pine green apron—the lower edge, the pocket, and the sash ends. Vertical threads are interwoven with triple stranded embroidery floss. The fourteen opposing pleats are anchored with X's and separated with a substantial V-shaped central design. What's truly amazing is that **all work is hand done**—hems, sashes, everything. This impresses me every time. $40-50.

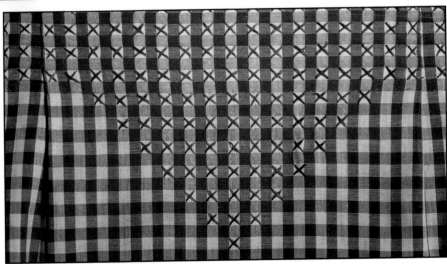

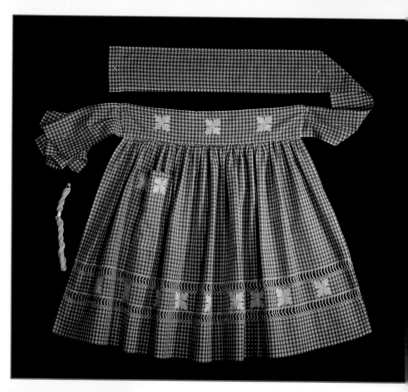

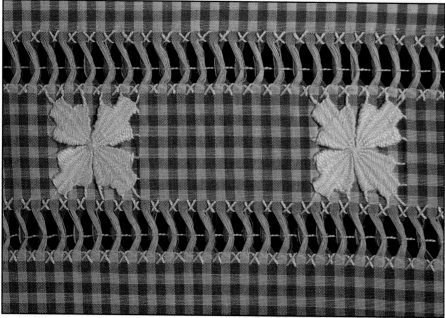

Fourteen luminescent Teneriffe designs capture the spotlight on this turquoise gathered apron. Glossy white pearl cotton is **the main ingredient** for all three embellishments—pulled thread, cross stitch, and Teneriffe lace. The pocket and waistband say 'me, too' with their own decorations. $30-40.

This eccentric yellow apron grabbed my attention more than once. I spotted it hanging from a cupboard door in an antique vendor's display. Seeing that the workmanship left plenty of **room for improvement**, I passed it by the first time. The second time I brought it home. I still wonder at the variety of not-so-carefully placed stitches and the myriad of embroidery colors. The maker has literally stretched cross stitches into elongated X's resembling feather stitching. Shades of pink, green, and blue clamor for attention. The drawn threads are grouped, but not interwoven, leaving them limp and ineffective. The twenty-four waistline pleats are uneven. None-the-less, all work is done by hand—an admirable feat under any circumstances. $30-40.

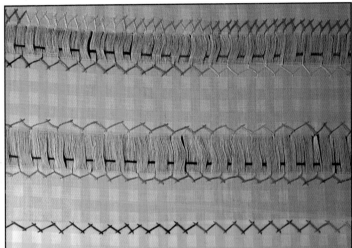

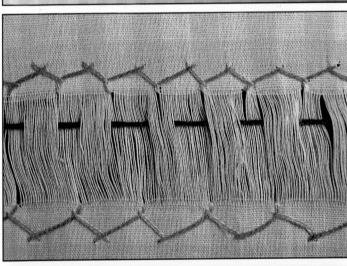

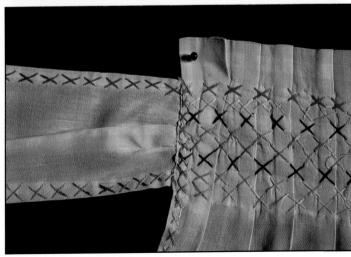

Just when I thought I'd seen every needlework technique used on gingham aprons, along came this intriguing specimen. In addition to cross stitches, uncrossed stitches, Teneriffe lace, and pulled thread, the maker of this pistachio green apron added **little brown woven circles** (each about the size and shape of a piece of toasted oat breakfast cereal). Each 'circle' is made from three strands of pearl cotton, woven through and anchored in the four corners with the contrasting color uncrossed stitches. The lower design is expansive (eight inches), and the pocket is peppered with all manner of needlework. *Courtesy of Betty Wilson. $40-50.*

Smocking

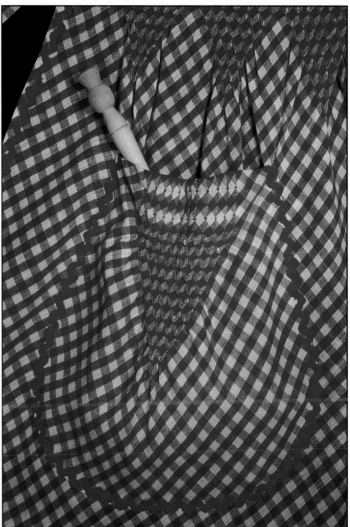

All eyes will be on the hostess wearing this fire engine red bias cut pear-shaped apron. The smocking alone is **a real attention getter**. Add to that the parallel rows of white diamonds created by tucking and the decorative red rickrack around the skirt and pocket. The four inch wide sashes are gathered at the waist and deeply angled at the ends. And 'huge' is the best word to describe the U-shaped pocket, which measures ten inches deep and eight inches at its widest part. $30-40.

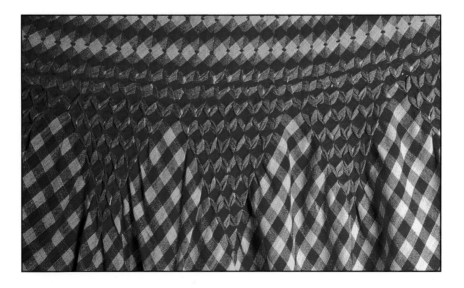

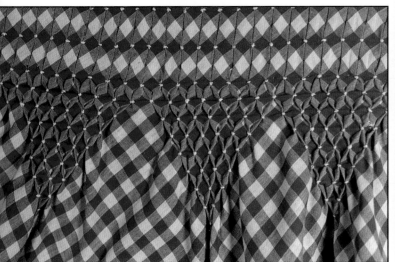

Equally impressive is this evergreen gingham apron with its sharply angled sides. Note these differences from the previous red apron: The white rickrack edge peaks from *behind* the fabric, secured with a double row of white top stitching, the pocket is smaller and rounder, and the sashes are narrower and pointed at the ends. The smocking is done with triple stranded white embroidery floss. All told, **exquisite design and detail**. $30-40.

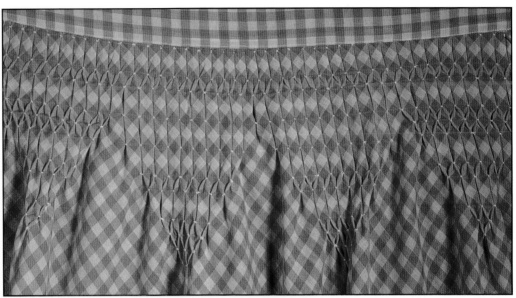

Smocking and tucking are the mainstays of this 1/4 inch lavender gingham. A generous observer might call this **an exercise in simplicity**. Others might label it 'lacking in detail'. Although the upper edge is liberally smocked using white pearl cotton, it's as if the maker then gave up. There are no trimmed edges. Each narrow sash is extended with 'make-do' piecing. And where in heck is the pocket? $20-30.

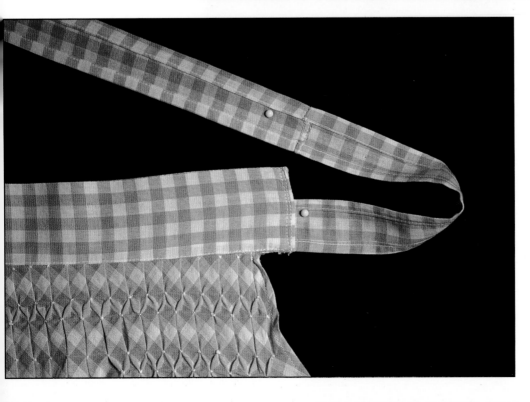

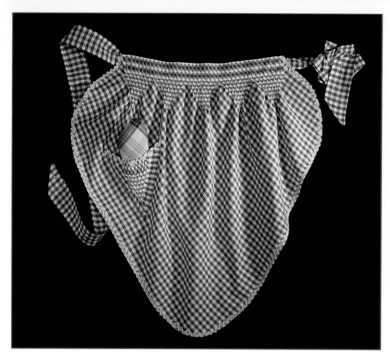

Look for **three unique features** on this blue smocked apron—the rounded and especially elongated shape of the skirt, the sharply pointed triangular pocket, and the dual colored rickrack. All smocking is hand done with double stranded white floss, and the rickrack is machine top-stitched in parallel rows of white thread. The acute angles of the patch pocket echo the shape of the upper smocked designs. *Courtesy of Terri Wyman.* $30-40.

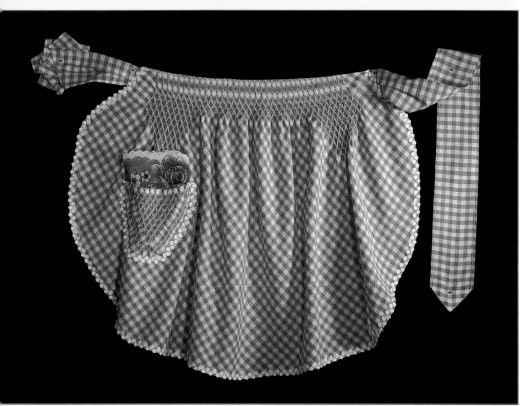

White rickrack and pink gingham make **a pleasing combination** on this broadly rounded design. The two smocked V's are widely separated by a band of tucks. Both the skirt and pocket edges are accented with white rickrack—all secured with hand stitches of lustrous pink pearl cotton. $30-40.

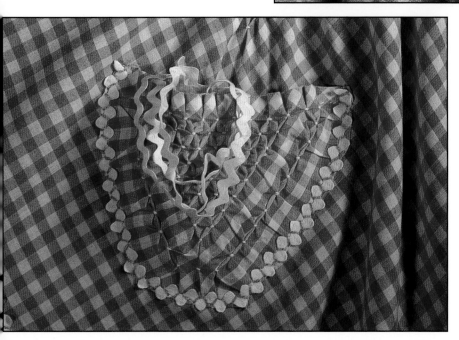

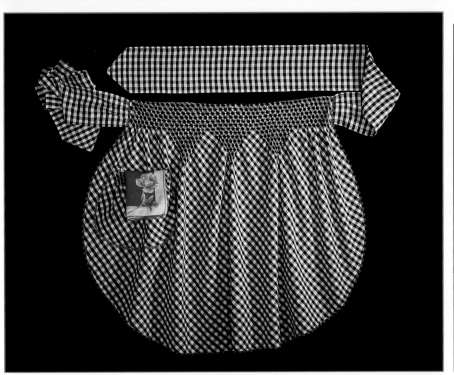

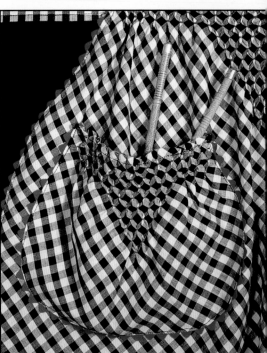

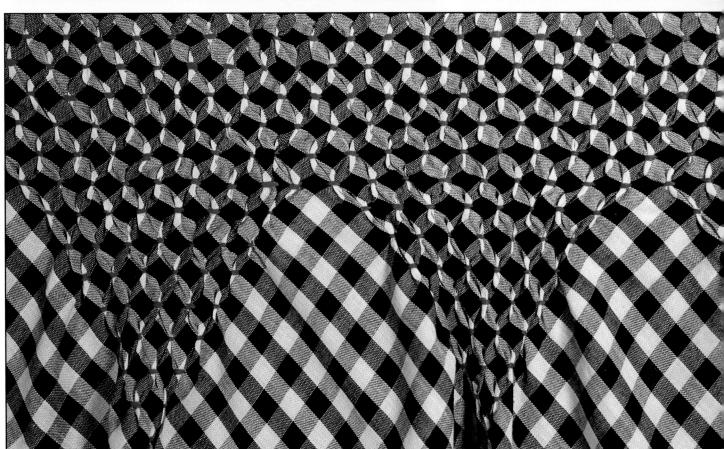

Red and black make a lovely combination—this time in red smocking, red rickrack, and black 1/4 inch gingham. The upper edge and the pocket are both lavishly smocked. The rickrack is secured from behind the skirt and pocket, with only one brightly colored edge peeking out. I especially like the spacious **pot-belly shaped pocket**. $30-40.

The previous six smocked aprons were all cut on the *bias* of the fabric, thus lending themselves to effective tucking and draping. The next two designs are cut from the *straight grain* of the fabric. Smocking works here, too, but it is not as impressive. The upper edge of this pink apron is smocked with black embroidery floss. It simply does not create the pleasing shapes or lay as agreeably as the smocking found on aprons cut from the bias. The maker filled the lower edge with loose boxy looking X's and horizontal running stitches. Not the finest in workmanship or design, but **good enough for the kitchen**. $20-30.

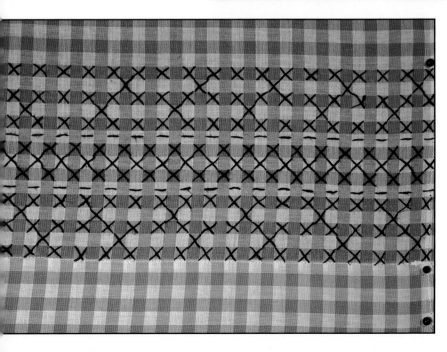

Having said that, here we have the most intricate and delicately smocked design in the book—and it is worked on th[e] *straight grain* of the fabric! But here's the difference. This smocking is worked on *1/8 inch* gingham; all previous aprons are on the wider 1/4 inch gingham. This design appears finer because it *is* finer. Furthermore, the smocking is executed with two colors of floss—burgundy and navy—and ornamented with multi-colored tiny ruched flowers. Truly **a work of art** on an otherwise ordinary apron. *Courtesy of Jan Holte.* $30-40.

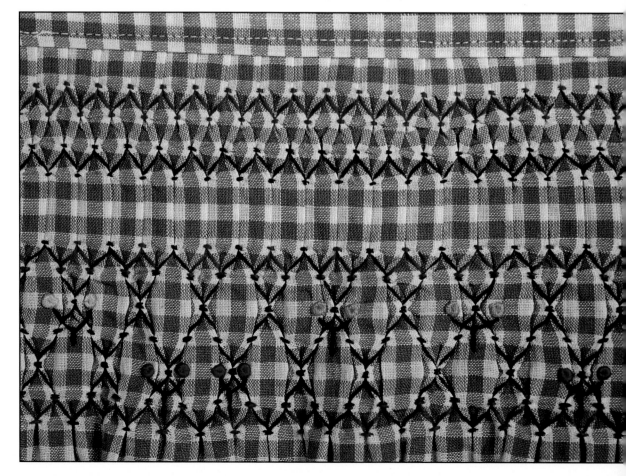

Teneriffe Lace

What a lovely **introduction to Teneriffe** design! Six dainty white designs grace the lower edge and pocket of this strawberry red apron. Each 5/8 inch design floats in a field of white uncrossed stitches. All embellishments are hand worked with triple stranded embroidery floss. The result—an immaculate and understated design that would be the pride of both maker and wearer. $30-40.

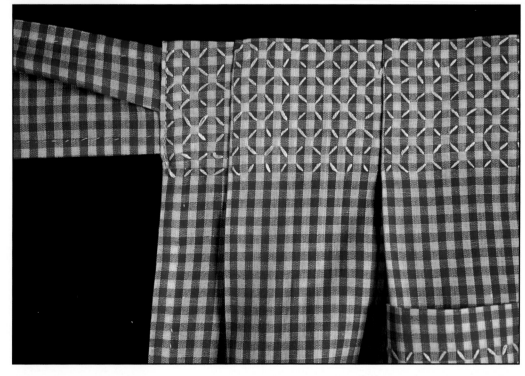

Slightly **more glitz and glamor** appear on this otherwise basic black gingham apron. Notice the mix of lustrous red and white pearl cotton used for the stitchery. Alternate placement of red and white Teneriffe designs, each accented with a cluster of contrasting French knots at the center, adds a showy accent to the border and pocket. The double cross stitches seem to glisten and sparkle like snowflakes or stars. $40-50.

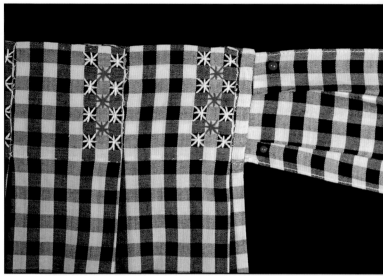

Emerald green Teneriffe takes the spotlight on this 1/8 inch gingham apron. The cross stitches along the border and pocket are oversize, each spanning four checks. The Teneriffe designs are also generous in size (1 3/8 inches). Both stitching and weaving are done with precision. The **trapezoidal groupings** of smaller cross stitches along the waistline lend a distinctive look to this apron. $30-40.

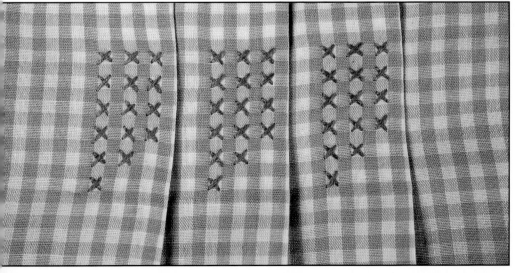

The next two aprons might be described as **fraternal twins**—obviously from the same pattern and by the same maker. Both are widely banded and thickly gathered using a cotton/polyester blended gingham. The navy blue design has embellishments of bright golden floss. The waistband, the pocket, and the lower edge of the skirt each receive similar attention. $30-40.

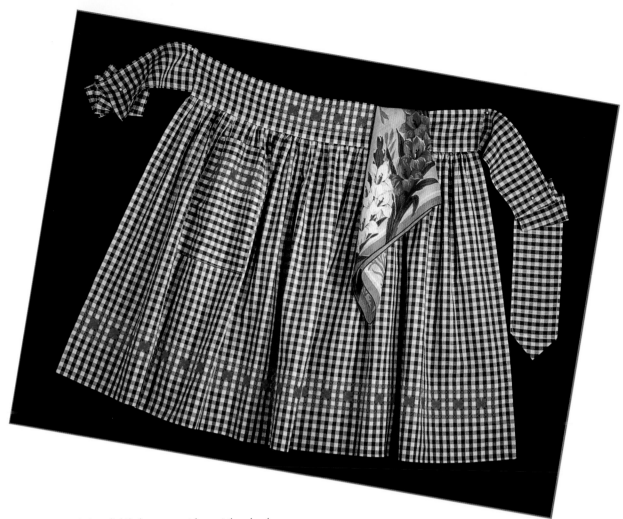

The **chocolate brown companion** is just slightly larger—a wider waistband, a longer skirt, and one more Teneriffe design in the border. Red may seem an unlikely choice with brown gingham, but each carefully woven Teneriffe design and crossed stitch looks just fine to me. $30-40.

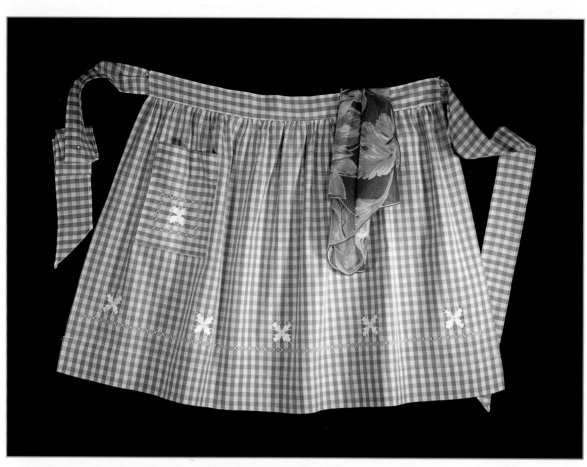

Five luminous Teneriffe designs float above a single row of cross stitches on this light green gathered apron. A solitary motif enclosed with X's accents the banded pocket. Each design is carefully woven with pearl cotton. Words like **modest and unpretentious** come to mind when describing this apron. $30-40.

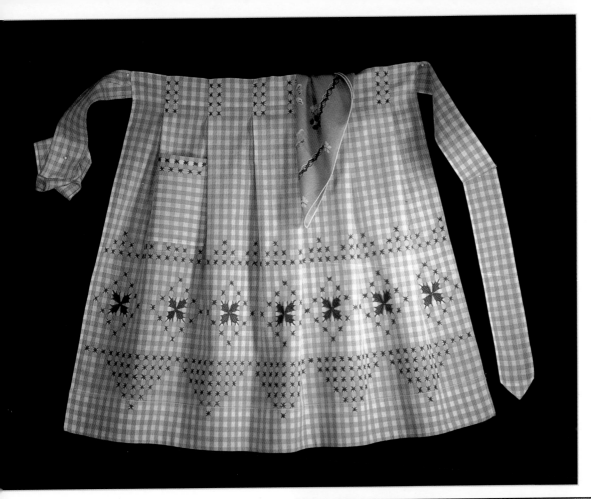

What one might have thought was lacking in the previous apron can likely be found on this peach colored design! In addition to the seven framed Teneriffe designs, we have triangle borders (in two sizes), a decorated pocket, and highlighted waistline pleats. All embroidery is done with triple stranded brown floss, and all X's are *double* cross stitched. Words like **dominant and excessive** come to mind. $30-40.

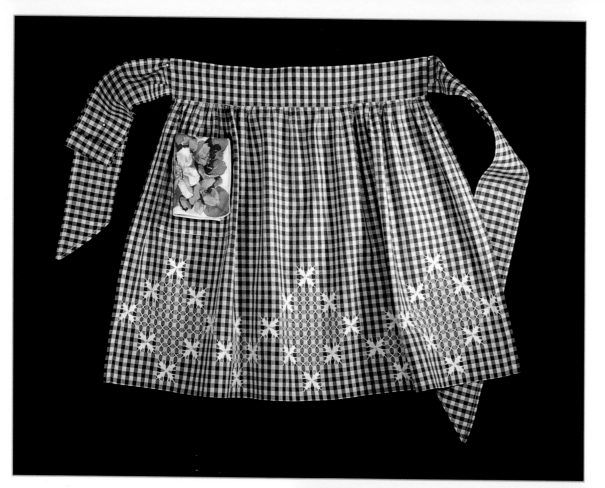

I always think 'evergreen' when I encounter a dark green apron. Maybe because as I write the captions for the aprons in this book, I frequently glance out the window at huge white pines. Often they are **snow laden evergreens**. How better to describe this green and white Teneriffe apron? Thirty-two snowflake-like designs grace the border. The interior cross stitches are worked in white pearl cotton. $30-40.

I nearly fainted when I discovered this colorful Teneriffe design in a Wisconsin antique mall. Twenty-four designs, and no two alike. Every color, tint, and shade has been woven into the patterns, using multi-colored cotton embroidery floss. Red and white *nearly* double cross stitches fill the background space and rise in triangles above the border. Similar red stitches enhance the pocket and waistline. Suitable descriptive words? How about **breathtaking and beautiful?** $40-50.

Stairstep Borders

Silver metallic rickrack, cross stitching with cross-bar filling, and golden Teneriffe—**this one has it all**, rendering it among the showiest of aprons in the book. The zigzag stairstep edge and on-point pocket add to the drama. Each large X is stitched with glossy white pearl cotton and accented with a golden center that matches the Teneriffe designs. You'll need more than three yards of metallic rickrack to meet the edging requirements of this forest green apron. $40-50.

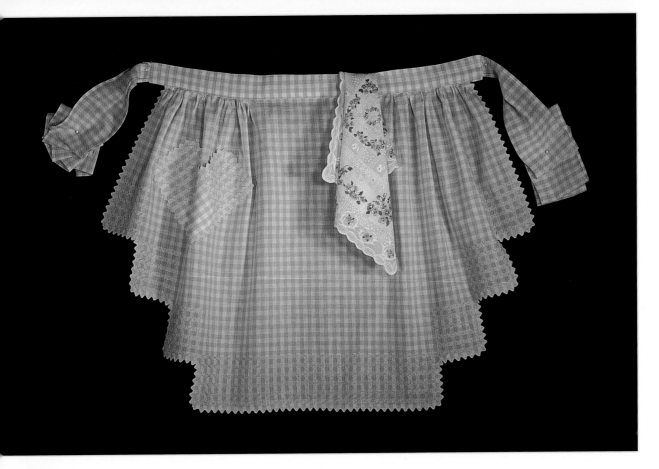

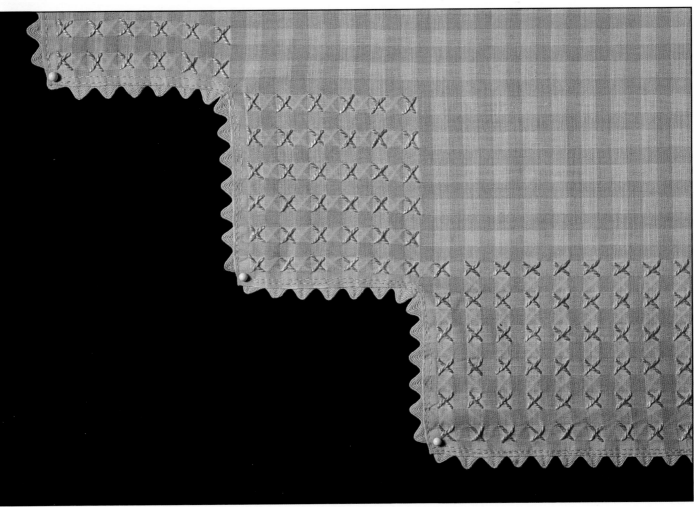

1/4 inch gingham, pearl cotton, and rickrack—all in the same pale pink—render this design nearly lifeless. But if pink is your favorite color (it's right up there with turquoise and red in the world of aprons), chances are you won't regard this as **an overdose of pink**. Instead, you'll appreciate the shiny cross stitches, the carefully attached rickrack edging, and the V-shaped pocket. $30-40.

Among the minority in the world of gingham aprons are the *printed* check designs. This 1/8 inch yellow fabric is crowded with tiny brown X's—more than twelve hundred—along the lower edge, on the pocket, and across the waistband. Cinnamon brown rickrack highlights the stairstep edges and the top of the pocket. *A gift from my son Dave.* $30-40.

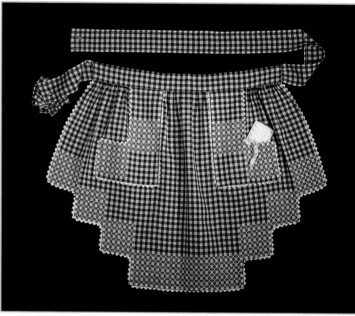

Brown gingham makes another appearance, this time with prominent X's stitched in white pearl cotton and distinctive drop-down pockets edged with white rickrack. It's **a simple formula**—clean lines, precision workmanship, and contrasting colors—leaving little room for improvement. $30-40.

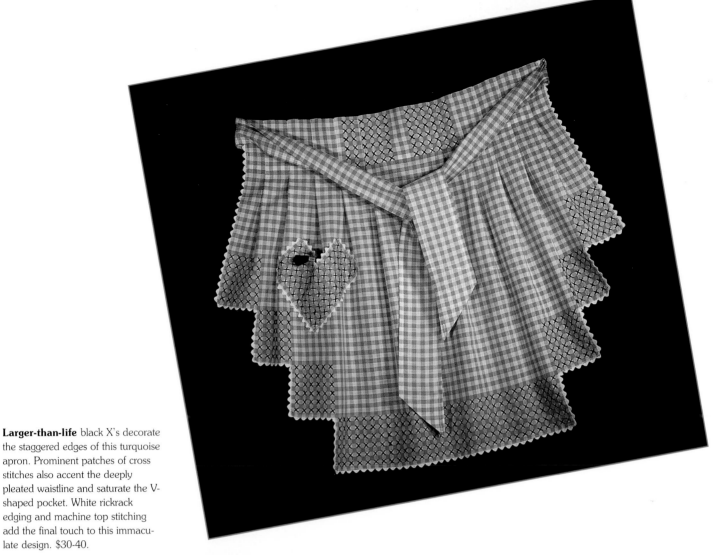

Larger-than-life black X's decorate the staggered edges of this turquoise apron. Prominent patches of cross stitches also accent the deeply pleated waistline and saturate the V-shaped pocket. White rickrack edging and machine top stitching add the final touch to this immaculate design. $30-40.

No, not another pink apron! But wait, here's something new, not to be found anywhere else in this book—eight commercial **white daisy decals**. Each flower is attached with pink floss, the same floss used for the tiny cross stitches. White rickrack is the right choice for pocket and outer edgings of this gathered design. $20-30.

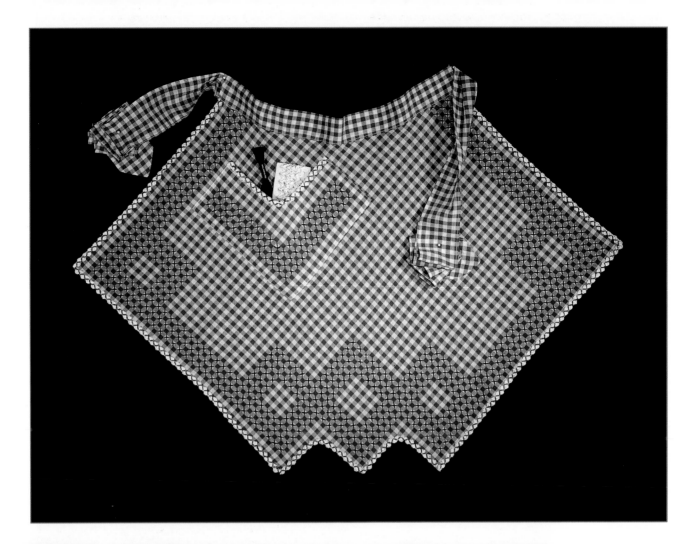

So what's unusual about this pea soup green number? 1) It is cut from the bias of the fabric. 2) It has no pleats nor gathers. 3) It has a true zigzag border. 4) It has an ever so carefully hand applied **golden rickrack edging.** 5) The oversize pocket neatly reflects the shape of the apron and outline of the lower edge. $30-40.

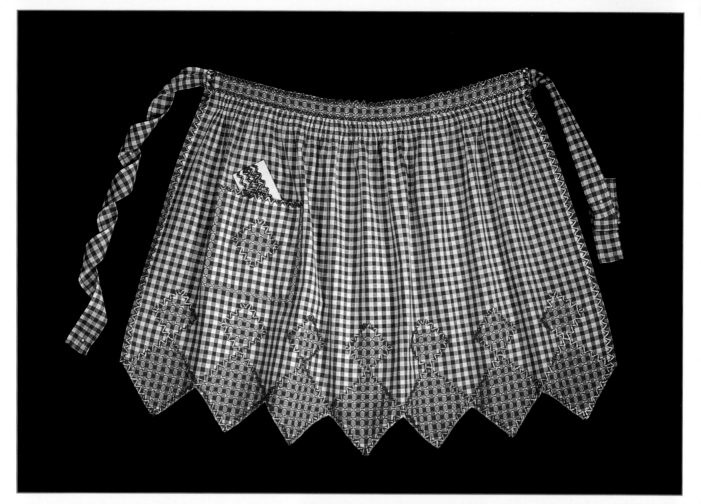

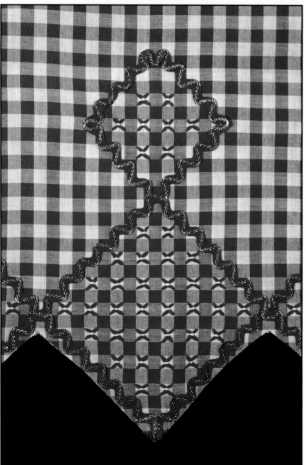

One might be accused of **saving the best for last** with this awesome fiery red apron. It is truly a mini master work of embellishments, including metallic rickrack, cross stitching with cross-bar filling, and a shirred waist. A substantial amount of rickrack will be needed. Also, include red and white embroidery floss on your list of supplies. Think back, have you seen a fancier pocket? $40-50.

In a Class by Themselves

Forest green gingham is the fabric of choice for this pentagonal **waitress style design**. The lower and side hems are entirely faced and accented with a 3/4 inch band of white cotton. This simplest of aprons is completed with three inch wide sharply pointed sashes. Hey, where's the pocket? $20-30.

Look no further! Here it is—the one and only apron (in *this* book) made from **1/2 inch gingham**. I purchased it at a resale shop in Wisconsin's fourth largest city. The store window prominently displayed a *75% discount on all clothing* sign. The original price was thirty-five cents, so the sale price was nine cents! (I have the receipt to prove it.) What pleased me most was finding the relatively rare 1/2 inch gingham. Never mind that the apron features a pleasing combination of cotton batiste and gingham, the waistband is slightly shaped, and the twin pockets and six mirrored pleats are so carefully placed. $30-40.

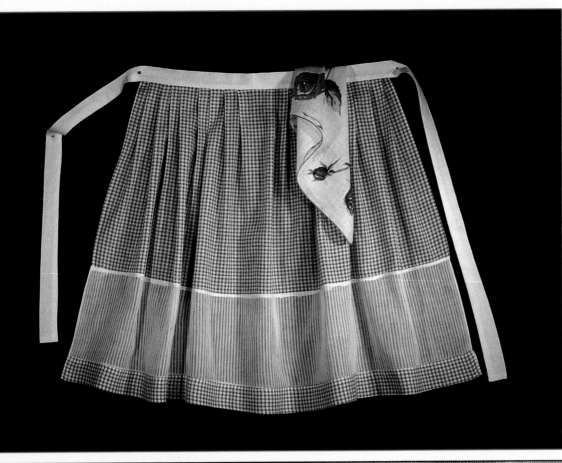

One of the few *printed gingham checks* in the book, this apron has an inset panel of plain white lightweight cotton. Sixteen opposing pleats top the skirt. The combination waistband/sash of cotton percale is pieced at the very center. $20-30.

149

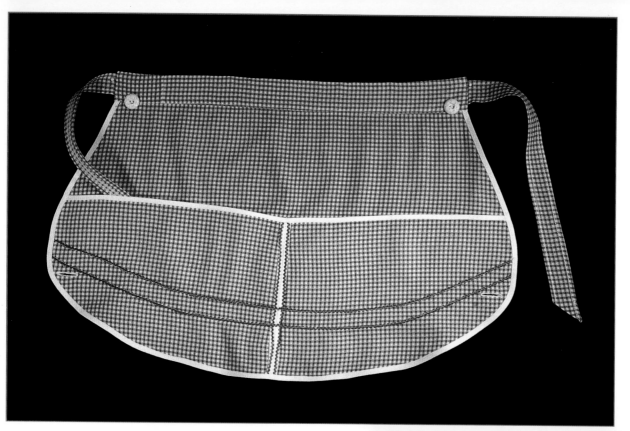

Rounded edges and generous pockets highlight this **gathering apron**. All edges are bound with white bias tape, and parallel rows of miniature blue rickrack provide the decoration. Two plastic white buttons and machine worked buttonholes give evidence that this apron can be cleverly converted into a sunbonnet. $20-30.

Not really gingham at all, this odd shaped apron utilizes a cotton print of mock check and floral bouquets. The perimeter is accented with a wide band of bright blue cotton, which transforms neatly into **weird shaped side pockets**. Pointed sashes and a slightly curved waistband top this factory made design. $20-30.

Among the most distinctive of gingham apron designs is this rare **combination of cross stitch and appliqué**. Six patterns have been stitched on colorful four inch squares and set on point in a chained border. Design details include a chicken, a butterfly, flowers, a heart, and geometric patterns, all hand stitched in assorted colors of embroidery floss. $40-50.

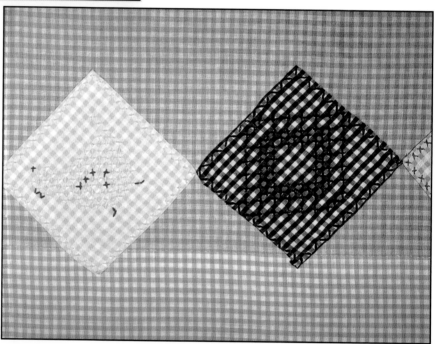

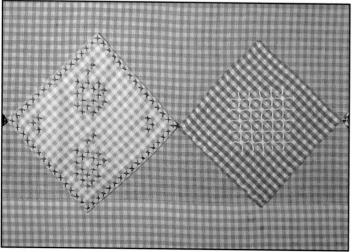

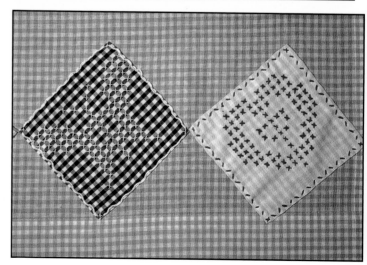

Once again, organdy and gingham pair up in a dramatic combination highlighted with cross stitching. The stairstep design includes two pockets and about **a gazillion tiny pink cross stitches** (over one thousand anyway). Miniature 1/4 inch pleats top the skirt of this oh-so-feminine design. $30-40.

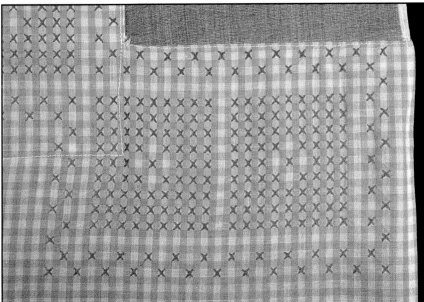

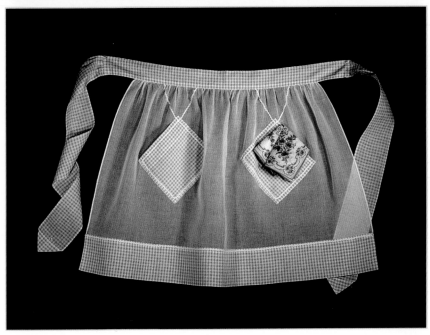

White cotton organdy prevails on this soft peach colored gingham apron. Paired patch pockets are **angled precariously** and anchored with miniature white rickrack, which drifts up into the gathered waist. Rickrack also accents the lower hem. $20-30.

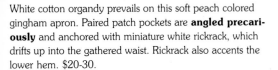

Add **hand crocheted edging** to the list of embellishments on gingham aprons—in this instance, a white scalloped edging on sunny yellow 1/4 inch checks. The outer edging is attached with dual rows of machine top-stitching. A generous drop down pocket is also edged with crochet, which continues up into the lightly gathered waistband. $20-30.

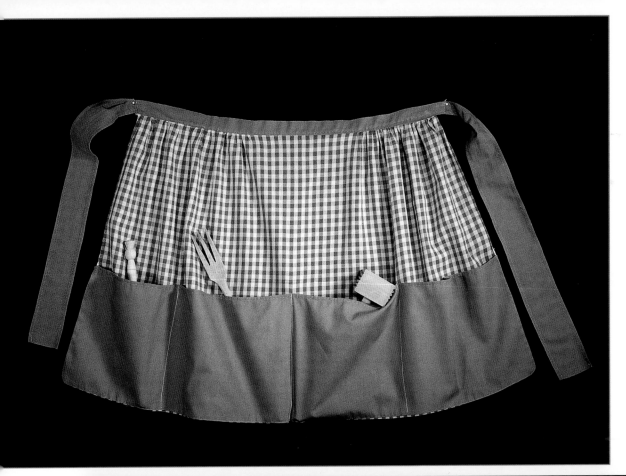

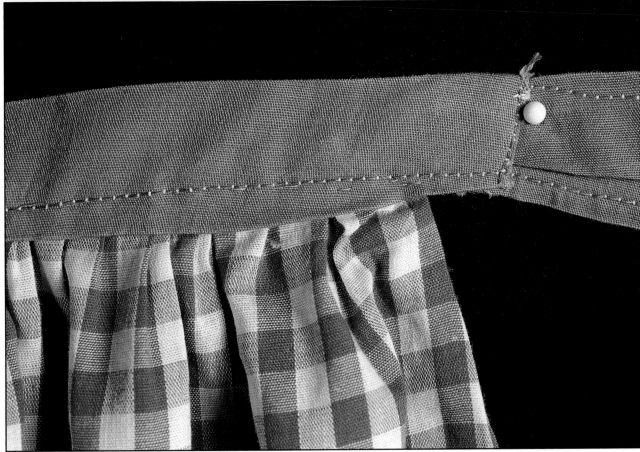

This cocoa brown apron is one of the most poorly constructed in the book. Uneven gathers, wavering waistband width, and crooked stitching lines are some of the infractions. Poor machine tension is evident—tiny dots of white bobbin thread peaking through the brown fabric. **Redeeming qualities** are the pleasing combination of the milk chocolate percale with 1/4 inch gingham and the four jumbo pockets. $10-20.

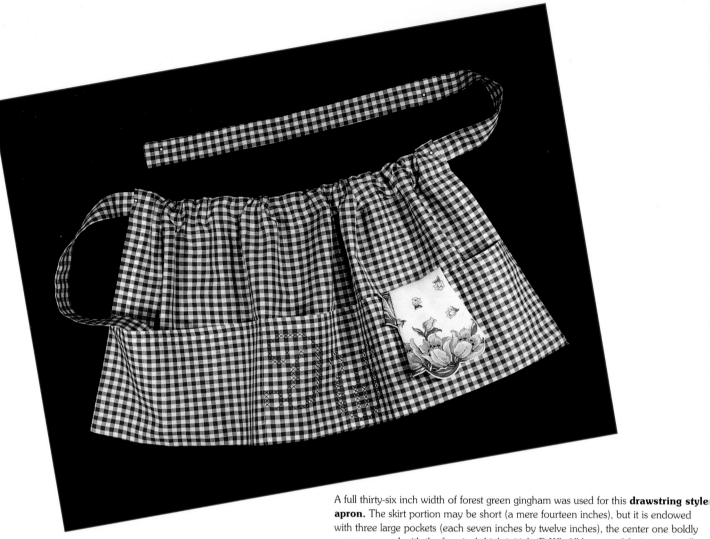

A full thirty-six inch width of forest green gingham was used for this **drawstring style apron.** The skirt portion may be short (a mere fourteen inches), but it is endowed with three large pockets (each seven inches by twelve inches), the center one boldly monogrammed with the four inch high initials 'D W'. All hems and facings are well secured with tiny, nearly invisible machine stitches. $20-30.

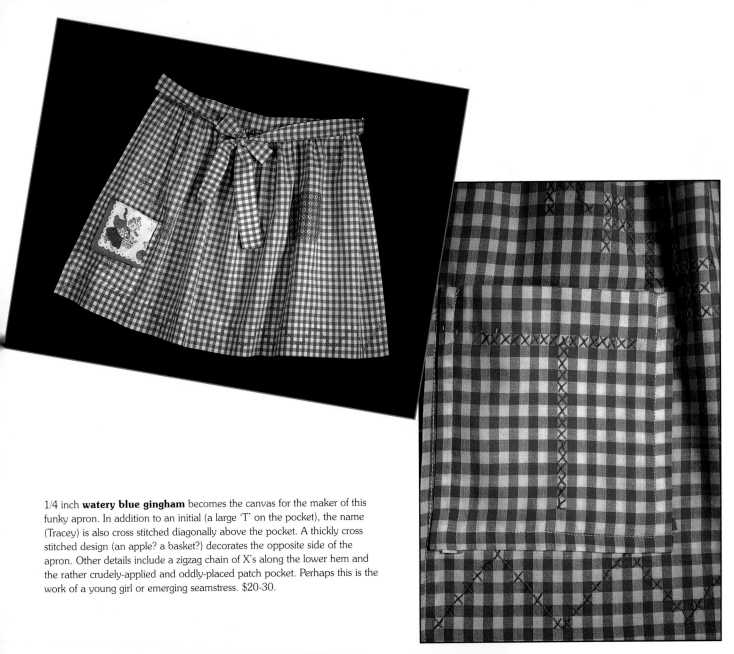

1/4 inch **watery blue gingham** becomes the canvas for the maker of this funky apron. In addition to an initial (a large 'T' on the pocket), the name (Tracey) is also cross stitched diagonally above the pocket. A thickly cross stitched design (an apple? a basket?) decorates the opposite side of the apron. Other details include a zigzag chain of X's along the lower hem and the rather crudely-applied and oddly-placed patch pocket. Perhaps this is the work of a young girl or emerging seamstress. $20-30.

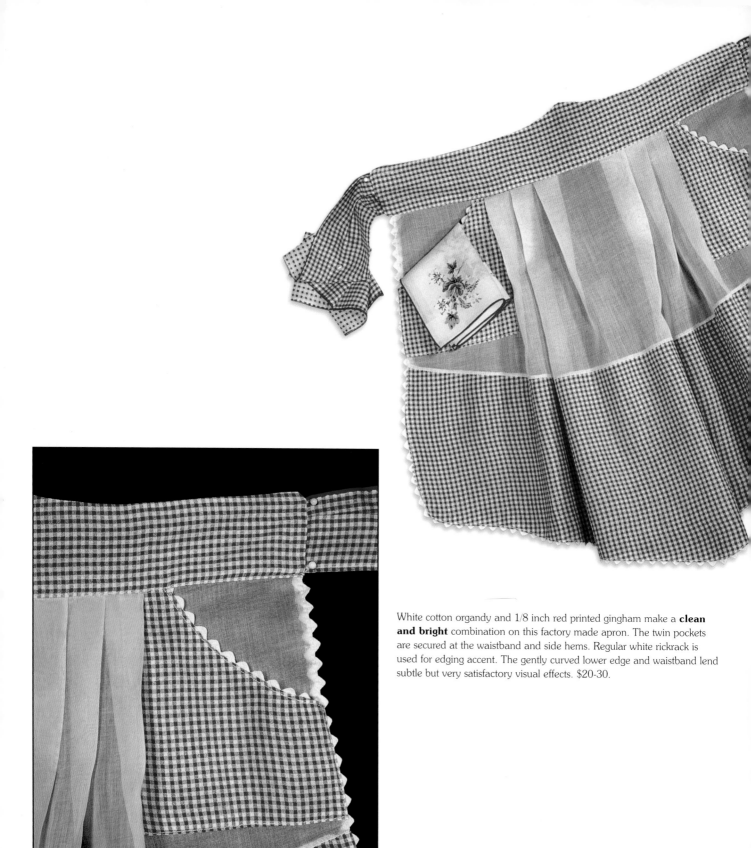

White cotton organdy and 1/8 inch red printed gingham make a **clean and bright** combination on this factory made apron. The twin pockets are secured at the waistband and side hems. Regular white rickrack is used for edging accent. The gently curved lower edge and waistband lend subtle but very satisfactory visual effects. $20-30.

A Word About Values

Most of the gingham aprons in this book are truly 'one-of-a-kind,' i.e., each was handmade by an individual, and there is no other apron exactly like it. Nearly all of them were made in the home (as opposed to factory made) and include some hand needlework. The majority are one hundred percent cotton and in excellent condition.

Placing a value designation on these aprons is unavoidably somewhat personal and arbitrary. I have studied and priced hundreds of aprons and have found that the most satisfactory method is to suggest a value 'range' rather than a specific price for each apron. Value designations are given in the ranges of $10-20, $20-30, $30-40, and $40-50.

I considered the following factors in assigning values:

1. **Condition** – Indications of wear or hard use, soil and stains, repeated launderings, and need for repairs decrease an apron's value.
2. **Fiber Content** – Natural fibers such as cotton and linen are more collectible. Aprons made from blends of cotton and polyester are usually less collectible (depending on other factors).
3. **Manufacturing Method** – Whether the apron was constructed by hand or by machine, and whether it was manufactured in the home or commercially (not always easy to ascertain) were considered. 'By hand' and 'in the home' usually carry greater value than 'by machine' or 'commercially made.'
4. **Embellishments** – The presence and amount of details such as cross stitching, rickrack trim, smocking, and pulled thread were considered, with greater value placed on the use of multiple techniques.
5. **Amount of Workmanship** – Whether the needle work was skimpy or elaborate was considered, the latter more valuable unless it detracted from the overall design.
6. **Quality of Workmanship** – The accuracy and consistency of both machine stitching and hand needlework were considered.
7. **Degree of difficulty** – More challenging designs received greater value than elementary efforts.
8. **Rarity** – If the color, fabric, design, or technique was highly unusual, greater value was assigned.

References

Anderson, Martha Lee. *Some of My Favorite Good Things to Eat* (Edition 129). New York: Church & Dwight Co., Inc., 1940.

Aunt Martha's Cross Stitch Designs #3558 and #3561. Kansas City, MO: Aunt Martha's Studios.

Baking is Fun . . . The Ann Pillsbury Way. Minneapolis, MN: Pillsbury Mills, Inc., 1945.

Better Homes & Gardens (and American Gas Company). Des Moines, IA: Meredith Corporation, March 1945.

Better Homes & Gardens. Des Moines, IA: Meredith Corporation, March 2001.

Carson, Byrta, and MaRue Carson Ramee. *How You Plan and Prepare Meals* (Second Edition). St. Louis, MO: Webster Division, McGraw-Hill Book Company, 1962 and 1968.

Eat and Grow. Minneapolis, MN: General Mills, Inc., 1946.

Elson, William H., and William S. Gray. *Elson-Gray Basic Readers, Book One.* Chicago: Scott, Foresman and Company, 1930 and 1936.

Florence, Judy. *Aprons of the Mid-20th Century: To Serve and Protect.* Atglen, PA: Schiffer Publishing, Ltd., 2001.

Good Things to Eat Made with Arm & Hammer Baking Soda. New York: Church & Dwight Co., Inc., 1933.

300 Helpful Suggestions for Your Victory Lunch Box. New York: Dell Publishing Co., Inc., 1943.

Hildreth, Gertrude. Illustrated by Corinne Pauli Waterall. *At Play* (Easy Growth in Reading). New York: The John C. Winston Company, 1940.

Home Baking Made Easy for Beginners and Experts. New York: Lever Brothers Company, 1953.

McCall's Printed Pattern #6664. The McCall Corporation.

Montgomery Ward. 1953 Spring/Summer Catalog. St. Paul, MN.

Montgomery Ward. 1956-57 Fall/Winter Catalog. St. Paul, MN.

O'Donnell, Mabel. *Down the River Road* (The Alice and Jerry Books). New York: Row, Peterson and Company, 1938.

O'Donnell, Mabel. *Through the Green Gate* (The Alice and Jerry Books). New York: Row, Peterson and Company, 1939.

Pollard, L. Belle. *Experiences with Foods.* Boston MA: Ginn and Company, 1956.

Quinlan, Myrtle Banks. Illustrations by Kayren Draper. *Day by Day* (The Quinlan Readers). Boston: Allyn and Bacon, 1939.

Recipes for Good Eating. The Proctor & Gamble Company, 1945.

Reed, Mary, and Edith Osswald. *Numbers: What They Look Like and What They Do* (A Little Golden Book). New York: Simon and Schuster, Inc., 1955.

Sears, Roebuck and Co. 1964 Fall and Winter Catalog. Minneapolis, MN.

Simplicity Printed Pattern # 4726. New York: Simplicity Pattern Co., Inc.

Taylor, Florence M. *Growing Pains.* Philadelphia: The Westminster Press, 1948.

The New Dr. Price Cook Book. Chicago: Royal Baking Powder Co., 1921.

Vogart Transfer Pattern # 127. New York: Vogart Co., Inc.

What Makes Jelly "Jell"? New York: General Foods Corporation, 1951.